T0267310

THE
POWER
OF
SELF

**HOW INSIGHT AND SELF-AWARENESS
LEAD TO YOUR AUTHENTIC SELF**

THE POWER OF SELF

OF

SELF

**HOW INSIGHT AND SELF-AWARENESS
LEAD TO YOUR AUTHENTIC SELF**

KEITH FLOYD, EdD

www.BookpressPublishing.com

Published in Des Moines, Iowa, by:

Bookpress Publishing
P.O. Box 71532, Des Moines, IA 50325
www.BookpressPublishing.com

Publisher's Cataloging-in-Publication Data

Names: Floyd, Keith, author.
Title: The Power of Self : How Insight and Self-Awareness Lead to Your Authentic Self / Keith Floyd, EdD.
Description: Des Moines, IA: Bookpress Publishing, 2024.
Identifiers: LCCN: 2022920224 | ISBN: 978-1-947305-59-5
Subjects: LCSH Business. | Success in business. | Strategic alliances (Business). | Business networks. | Interorganizational relations. | Cooperation. | Competition. | BISAC BUSINESS & ECONOMICS / Organizational Development
Classification: LCC HD69.S8 .M34 2023 | DDC 338.8--dc23

First Edition
Printed in the United States of America
10 9 8 7 6 5 4 3 2 1

For all of my family, friends, colleagues, and clients who made this lifelong dream possible by way of, and through the means of, your love, encouragement, support, and instruction. I am eternally grateful to each and every one of you and wish to thank you from the bottom of my heart.

CONTENTS

OPENING

A MASTERCLASS IN
SELF-AWARENESS & AUTHENTICITY

On Thursday, May 1, 1969, a slender-built 41-year-old gentleman in a neatly pressed dark suit sat on the far side of a large, sturdy, rectangular, brown conference table, strategically placed before a panel of committee members.[1] On this day, this unimposing man from Pennsylvania was about to present his testimony before the Senate Subcommittee on Communications. The subcommittee had been tasked with gathering information and insights pertaining to proposed budget cuts that would amount to a fifty percent reduction in the total annual operating budget of the fledgling (govern-ment-funded) broadcasting company. This was now the third day of testimony before the committee and its influential chairman. The committee chairman was Senator John Pastore, a slight but imposing figure. The son of Italian immi-grants, he came from nothing and rose through the political ranks—first within the Rhode Island legislature, then to the governorship of Rhode Island, to eventually becoming the first Italian American elected to the United States Senate. During his nearly twenty-year tenure in the Senate (to that point), Senator Pastore had gained a reputation for railing against television as a whole, which made these hearings and proceedings even more challenging.[2]

As the man from Pennsylvania prepared to address Senator Pastore and the committee, he recalled learning of the Senator's growing displeasure with the sheer volume of well-crafted and well-rehearsed statements by each of the previous witnesses over the course of the previous two days. Each statement espoused the value, merit, and worth of the fledgling broadcasting company and the need for its con-tinued existence. As the man moved closer to the micro-phone, he was introduced as a recent Peabody Award winner, which is the equivalent of the Pulitzer Prize for excellence in broadcasting—a fact that would hopefully add some credi-bility to his testimony.

The witness began by sharing that he, too, had prepared a philosophical statement that was very important to him and would take about ten minutes to read. Wanting to respect the Senator's wishes, he chose not to read his prepared remarks, instead trusting that the chairman and the committee would read the statement at a later date (as promised) and instead began to speak to his statement and from his heart. He began by sharing his concern for children and what they see and hear on television—much akin to Senator Pastore's own personal beliefs.[3] He shared that his program dealt with real topics and challenges that children experience—like getting a haircut or their feelings about brothers and sisters, as well as many more within the breadth of his programming.

As the soft-spoken witness continued to speak and to share how others had described his show as a "neighborhood expression of care," Senator Pastore listened intently, as well as asked questions about the show—even requesting to have a copy of an episode made available to him to view at some point in the near future. As the heartfelt testimony continued, the witness shared how he gave "an expression of care, each day, to every child" by helping them to realize that they are unique, as well as making it clear to them that it's okay to talk about their feelings and to be able to control their emotions. He then went on to share how beneficial it would be for two adults (men) to be able to work out their anger and differences with something other than a fury of gunfire and instead be able to utilize what they had learned as children.

At that moment, the chairman shared that he was emotionally moved for the first time in two days by the witness's testimony. Honored by the emotional impact he (the witness) had made and what that meant to the children that he served, he asked to share one final thought pertaining to a child being able to demonstrate personal control by sharing the lyrics to a song that he had written and performed on his program—thoughts and actual words given to him by a child:

> *What do you do with the mad that you feel? When you feel so mad you could bite. When the whole wide world seems oh so wrong, and nothing you do seems very right. What do you do? Do you punch a bag? Do you pound some clay or some dough? Do you round up friends for a game of tag or see how fast you go? It's great to be able to stop when you've planned the thing that's wrong. And be able to do something else instead — and think this song —*

> *I can stop when I want to. Can stop when I wish. Can stop, stop, stop anytime ... And what a good feeling to feel like this! And know that the feeling is really mine. Know that there's something deep inside that helps us become what we can. For a girl can be someday a lady, and a boy can be someday a man.*[4]

Immediately following the last words of the lyrics to the song, Pastore stated, "I think it's wonderful, I think it's wonderful." He then proceeded to announce that the witness had just earned full funding for the broadcasting company and that the proposed cuts would not occur.

The lesson of (and in) the all but six-minute heartfelt testimony before the Senate Subcommittee on Communications from this impassioned and caring man demonstrated the power of opening himself up and sharing with the world (or, in this case, a prominent, commanding Senator from Rhode

Island and his fellow committee members) his true self. His *authentic* self. And in doing so, he changed the course of the Public Broadcasting Service (PBS)—saving it from the brink of near extinction even before it had truly begun to flourish. In addition, this humble man was able to continue his mission: to teach millions upon millions of children and adults (even the now-adult penning this book) that we are unique, special, and have much to give. And who was this gentle yet impassioned witness who changed the course of public broadcasting and the world? None other than Mr. Rogers. Fred Rogers' vision, care, and compassion showed the world on a somewhat non-descript day in May 1969 that being your "authentic self" can change the mind of one (Senator John Pastore), as well as enlighten, enrich, teach, and even change the course of (and for) others by simply being you and inviting those around you into "your neighborhood."

But how did he do it? How did he know what to say? And more importantly, how did he know how to say it? The answers to these questions are quite simple, while also being simplistically complex. He did it by knowing who he was and what he believed in, and most importantly, he was able to articulate these parts of himself to others by both his words and actions.

This knowledge of self (one's true self) is what we will explore in this book by means of *The Power of Self*. Specifically, authenticity. But what is authenticity? What does it mean to be authentic? What components and insights do we need to have within us and at our command? And if these insights about ourselves are not yet known and still need to be discovered–how do we go about doing so? This is what you will learn, and we will explore it together in the pages that follow. We will discover that authenticity comes from knowing who you are—your strengths, your blind spots, and your contributions through *The Power of Self-Knowledge*. From there, we will explore how and why you are the way you are. Specifically, becoming enlightened about how and why you think that way and how your thinking guides you. This enlightenment will be accomplished by means of *The Power of Self-Concept*. And lastly, we will explore and determine what you stand for—your causes, your beliefs, and your guiding purpose (or "why") in life through *The Power of Self-Understanding*.

When joined together and in concert, these three explorations are powerful resources that will guide you as a person, a leader, a co-worker, a parent, and even a friend. The outward extension of these three enlightenments opens you up to the world and allows the world to gain access to who you are and what you believe. It brings us together and connects us to those who are the recipients of our authentic self, just like Mr. Rogers did on that non-descript day in May of 1969.

SELF: PART 1

KNOW WHO YOU ARE:
THE POWER OF SELF-KNOWLEDGE

"The greatest gift you ever give is your honest self."
- Fred Rogers

"Who are you?" Three simple words, one simple question. Or is it? On the surface, the first and obvious answer is actually quite simple: "I'm [insert your name here]." But that's not the real question here, is it? This question, in the context of this book, is intended to go much deeper and make you ponder who you really are. Better yet, do you actually know, and do you have an answer to this simple three-word question? Based upon my personal and professional experiences, I would speculate that you may never have given this simple question the deep thought and consideration that it fully deserves. As to why you haven't, I believe that answer is grounded in one, two, or all three of the following core reasons.

CORE REASON 1

The first reason for this hesitancy is that it is uncomfortable, even downright terrifying, to be asked such a deeply personal question. In answering such a question, you open yourself up to the world and lay yourself bare. It's frightening to share with others what you believe, what you're passionate about, how you see things, how you think about things, and how all of this comes together to make you, you. But is it really? Or should it be?

CORE REASON 2

The second reason is that your answer to the question is more than likely so large, so complex, and so multifaceted that it becomes almost too overwhelming to even think about—let alone to try to put your response into the context of a few words. But it can be done. It has been done. Mr. Rogers did it (and more) in a little more than six minutes before the Senate subcommittee. The ease with which Fred Rogers spoke so personally and passionately about his beliefs, principles, and his calling was due to the fact that he had taken the time to engage in deep self-reflection and introspection.[5] On that day and all the days that followed, he had the self-knowledge, self-concept, self-understanding, and most importantly, the emotional intelligence to connect with Senator Pastore, the committee members, and, perhaps more importantly, with his own inner self. This *inner self* is where you will spend your time throughout this book. Taking the time and giving the attention to dig deep into the confines of you—who you are, how you see and process things, how you see and understand others, as well as how you navigate within and around this world and your life, all due to the construct of who you are.

CORE REASON 3

The third and final reason is that of commitment. Your commitment. Your commitment to willingly dig in and around the innermost parts of yourself and to gather these pieces of you, all-the-while pulling these discoveries and insights together in a meaningful and useful way.

This notion of commitment leads to the next more direct question: "Do you have the desire, and most importantly, the wherewithal to search for and bring these core parts of you to the surface and into the light of day?" This is a question that *only you* can answer. But before you answer, one quick disclaimer: this journey and the following exercises will take some time, thought, and willingness to swim in and around your own head, as well as the courage to enlist others to join you on your journey of self-discovery. If this prospect seems too daunting or too scary, realize that there is a reward at the end of each of these discoveries. The reward is *enlightenment*, and, more than likely, a sense of clarity—perhaps for the first time in your life—as to who you truly are and what you have to contribute to this life. In addition to the discoveries, you will have also gained access and insight into the best ways to demonstrate your authentic self to those around you. Additionally, through the enlistment and assistance of honest and reliable partners within your circle of trust, you will more than likely gain an even deeper connection with each of these individuals and, in the process, establish even stronger, longer-lasting bonds with one another. But to allow all of this to occur, you must first know yourself.

According to multiple historians, there was once an inscription at the entrance to the courtyard of the Temple of Apollo at Delphi in Greece, which read ΓΝΩΘΙ ΣΑΥΤΟΝ, which translates from the ancient Greek to "Know Thyself."[6] This simple yet profound statement is timeless and universal in both its meaning and its intent, especially when you consider that the current ruins of the Temple of Apollo date back to between 300-400 BCE, meaning that man's quest for self-knowledge can be traced back nearly 2,500 years, and most likely even longer. As you begin to explore your own personal viewpoints, be comforted by the fact that countless others have undertaken this same exploration over the course of the last several millennia, including the likes of Socrates, Plato, and Aristotle—the greats of Greek philosophy.[7] Hence, you are in very good company!

To begin this discovery, it is important to first define the word *self-knowledge*. Self-knowledge, in the simplest terms, is what you know about yourself. In short, what aspects of you make you—*you*? And more importantly, are you aware of these aspects, and do you acknowledge these facets of yourself? Realize that this sense of self-knowledge is one of the greatest enlightenments (among many) that you will ever possess and is paramount to being and becoming the person that you are truly meant to be—your authentic self. Take a moment to think about and reflect upon the last statement. If you are truly looking to become your authentic self, you must be willing to be one hundred percent honest with yourself as you assess each and every part of you. In addition, you must be willing to not only accept your own revelations but also consider the insights and feedback that others gift to you, either by your direct request of them throughout the course of this book or by what they have told you at some point in the past. This intersection of self-acknowledgment and personal feedback leads to the next question that you must consider and answer before moving forward.

The next question is, "Will your journey be one of isolation–meaning that you are planning on doing this on your own and without any help or assistance, or will you bring other trusted colleagues, friends, and family into the fold during your journey of discovery?" This question is so important because when you look inward or utilize the process of *introspection*, you can gain great insight about yourself. But when you couple that with the help of others, gaining their insights and feedback, and taking a more *interpersonal* approach, the power and depth of the knowledge gained can be nearly immeasurable.[8] Immeasurable for sure, but also at times potentially uncomfortable because there may very well be aspects of yourself—shortcomings, weaknesses, or blind spots—that are not as flattering as you would hope. This feedback can be difficult to hear and acknowledge, but receiving it is also incredibly important, for instance, feedback containing new information about yourself that you may have inadvertently overlooked or have even purposefully chosen not to acknowledge in the first place. In either case, the depth of insight that can be gained from this intersection of introspection and interpersonal feedback can be absolutely life-changing. But how do you make this happen? How do you elicit, gather, and document such powerful and enlightening information? To do so, you will need some tools.

TOOL 1: A WAY TO COLLECT YOUR INSIGHTS AND FEEDBACK

The easiest and most effective way to collect your and others' insights and feedback during this journey is to simply write it down. To assist with this task and to get you started, refer to Figure 1.1, or go to *www.ThePowerofSelfbook.com* where you will find downloadable PDF versions of this chart, as well as all other forms and documents used throughout this book. In addition, and as you will see, there are also areas embedded throughout this book that will allow you to capture the insights, feedback, and learnings directly into the book itself, thus creating a workable journal or blueprint for harnessing *The Power of Self.*

| **Your Name:** _____ The Power of *Self* |
| Date: _____ |

Strengths	**B**lind Spots	**C**ontributions
Self:	Self:	Self:
Others:	Others:	Others:

Figure 1.1

TOOL 2: A WAY TO CAPTURE YOUR INSIGHTS AND FEEDBACK

One of the tools or methods that you can use to gain both your personal and interpersonal feedback is one that I have coined as *The 3-Words Method*. *The 3-Words Method* is incredibly simple in its construct, but at the same time, unbelievably insightful when used in either a personal aspect or when eliciting insights and feedback from others. The method works like this. When you are confronted with an idea, issue, question, or event (say contemplating your areas of respective strengths, blind spots, or contributions and beyond), or you don't know what to make of a circumstance, or you are at some type of impasse—simply ask yourself (or others) for the first three words that come to mind regarding the given question or circumstance and capture it by writing it down. The reasoning behind the first three words that come to mind and the significance of the words given will be explained more fully in a moment.

TOOL 3: A WAY TO "DIG DEEPER" INTO YOUR INSIGHTS AND FEEDBACK

One of the final tools at your disposal is to simply give yourself permission to slow down, pause, and engage in quiet (uninterrupted) deep thought and reflection about the insights and feedback that you've acquired through reflection or received from others. We live in an incredibly noisy world full of distractions—distractions that invade every corner of our world on a minute-by-minute, even second-by-second basis. Allowing yourself the time and attention to reflect and learn by giving yourself the permission to slow down and think is nearly a lost art. Additionally, as you reflect and learn, you must also give yourself one additional concession along this journey: the concession of *grace*. Grace to learn about the best and worst parts of yourself. Grace to receive feedback about the best and worst parts of yourself from others. Grace to process it all without being self-deprecating, but instead granting yourself some grace to take it all in and to learn from it—allowing yourself to truly be on the path to becoming the next best version of yourself.

The three reasons laid out at the onset of this chapter,

along with the three tools, their methods, and the constructs just outlined, will be the foundational starting points to exploring your strengths, your blind spots, and your respective contributions.

YOUR STRENGTHS

The first stage of introspection and interpersonal feedback is the area of personal strengths. Strengths are what you are good, confident, and successful at doing. Or if enlisting assistance from others, what do they perceive or have they witnessed you demonstrating that could be interpreted as being a respective area of strength?

To accomplish this first introspection task, I urge you to utilize the tools outlined in the preceding pages, with one additional piece of advice and guidance to consider—how it aligns with *The 3-Words Method*. As you start exploring the things that you do well (your respective strengths), as well as your upcoming reflections on your respective blind spots, contributions, and beyond, the challenge will be to write down the very first three words that come into your mind. For example, my strengths are that I am (a):

• Listener

• Student

• Compassionate

In capturing these words, try not to ponder or take too long contemplating the given aspect of yourself. The reason for this initial reaction is that this response, or your instant *gut reaction*, tends to be the most accurate on almost every occasion. If you spend too much time contemplating, you tend to either overthink or over- (or under-) inflate your appraisal. For example, my overinflated strengths are that I am a/an:

- Fixer (instead of Listener)
- Expert (instead of Student)
- Counselor (instead of Compassionate)

Or, in capturing your words, you do the converse and overthink and then under-inflate your appraisal. For example, my strengths are that I am (a):

- Quiet (instead of a Listener)
- Beginner (instead of Student)
- Bleeding-heart (instead of Compassionate)

In either case, each, in turn, tends to either jeopardize or even negate the accuracy of your self-assessment. This fact (the accuracy of your personal assessment) is yet another reason and benefit for eliciting the assistance of others who know you well as you explore the various aspects of yourself.

The interpersonal approach, or the utilization and assistance from others to broaden your self-assessment during this exploration, works best when you recruit individuals who know you well. Still, it is also important to enlist individuals who know you in a variety of different aspects of your life. Meaning intimate friendships, for instance, spouse, partner, family member, or very close friends, and based upon your level of relationship and comfort, certain business colleagues, and clients. This cross-section of personal and professional confidants will truly give you a deep and rich base of observed strengths that will be a great complement to your own personal assessment, especially if the confidants provide you with *strength words* that are not listed by you or better yet fall within the realm of an undiscovered strength that currently resides within an unexplored area or blind spot—a topic that we will explore momentarily.

Answer and chart your initial responses to the two questions that follow utilizing either the chart from Figure 1.1, the downloaded PDF from *The Power of Self* website, or Exercise 1.1 below, in conjunction with *The 3-Words Method*.

 ## 3-WORDS: **SELF**

- What three words best describe your
  top three **PERSONAL STRENGTHS**?

  1. _____

  2. _____

  3. _____

- What three words best describe your
  top three **PROFESSIONAL STRENGTHS**?

  1. _____

  2. _____

  3. _____

Exercise 1.1

With these initial introspection strengths tasks now completed, determine, contact, and enlist (if you have not already done so) a cross-section of family members, close friends, colleagues, and confidants to provide you with their insights about your respective strengths, and then chart their responses to the following questions in Exercise 1.2.

 # 3-WORDS: **OTHERS**

- What three words best describe my
  top three **PERSONAL STRENGTHS?**

1. _____   1. _____   1. _____

2. _____   2. _____   2. _____

3. _____   3. _____   3. _____

Name:_____   Name:_____   Name:_____

- What three words best describe my
  top three **PROFESSIONAL STRENGTHS?**

1. _____   1. _____   1. _____

2. _____   2. _____   2. _____

3. _____   3. _____   3. _____

Name:_____   Name:_____   Name:_____

Exercise 1.2

Staying within the confines and realm of strengths, another resource that is tremendously helpful and specifically geared toward personal strengths, and one that I have found to be an immensely valuable tool in the pursuit of identifying individual strengths, is the *StrengthsFinder 2.0* assessment.[9] The *StrengthsFinder 2.0* assessment was created by Dr. Donald Clifton via the Gallup Organization in association with Tom Rath—the same Gallup Organization that runs all of those polls. The assessment was developed utilizing a vast amount of data and is (in my opinion) a wonderfully accurate assessment and tool. The power of *StrengthsFinder* is that it is singularly focused on identifying the known and unknown strengths (blind spots) of the person taking the assessment. The assessment is based upon Dr. Clifton's research and Tom Rath's work. Through their respective work, they have identified and categorized 34 separate and distinct strength areas. These areas cover everything from the *Achiever*, people who work hard and take "great satisfaction from being busy and productive," to Woo, people who "love the challenge of meeting new people and winning them over."[10] These are just two of the categorized strength areas, with all manner of other strengths housed in between.

There is a fee to gain access to the assessment. You will need to purchase an access code at either the Gallup website (https://store.gallup.com/h/en-us) or through the purchase of the *StrengthsFinder 2.0* book itself, which contains a one-time-use access code at the back of the book. Once the online assessment is completed, which takes about 35-45 minutes in total and should be completed in one uninterrupted session, you will receive a personalized report that contains your top five personal strengths (in rank order from greatest strength to lesser strength), as well as insights into how to understand and even grow these strengths even further. There is also one other additional benefit to this assessment that will assist you with your next assignment, which is to identify and list your respective blind spots. The *StrengthsFinder* online portal allows you to purchase the full ranking of your results (the total list of 34 themes) in complete rank order for a nominal cost. This full report provides you with your lesser-developed strengths or weaker areas, which will lead nicely into our next area of exploration, your respective blind spots.

Take the *StrengthsFinder 2.0* assessment utilizing either the website link and access code or the link and access code from the back of the book *StrengthsFinder 2.0 From Gallup: Discover Your CliftonStrengths* book. Upon completion of the assessment, download and print out the personalized report with your top five strengths or print out the complete inventory of 34 strengths (for an additional fee) and review and report the findings below.

 ONLINE RESOURCE: **TOP 5 STRENGTHS**

1. _____

2. _____

3. _____

4. _____

5. _____

Exercise 1.3 (Optional)

Consider the totality of your collected strengths data to this point, your personally generated list of strengths, the lists of words and feedback gained from your family, friends, colleagues, and confidants through the use of *The 3-Words Method*, as well as your results from the purchased assessment (if this resource was utilized). Take some time to look at and review each piece of data carefully. Utilizing Tool 3 from the onset of this chapter, pause and reflect on the totality of the data collected and what it says about you. While doing so, remember to grant yourself the permission of time to *dig deep* and do some deep reflection while also using the concession of *grace* when you review and answer the following questions in Reflection 1.1.

 **REFLECTION**

1. What's resonating with you, or landing on you, based upon the collected data and your respective results?

_____

_____

_____

_____

_____

2. Were there any surprises? If so, what were they?

_____

_____

_____

_____

_____

3. What will you do with either the affirmations or unexpected
   insights gained through these exercises?

_____

_____

_____

_____

_____

Reflection 1.1

There is much to be gained from not only looking inward,
but by also enlisting the assistance of others (personal and
professional confidants), as well as the assistance of other
tools and resources (*StrengthsFinder 2.0*). The combination
of these deeply personal insights and feedback, along with the
research-based and professionally curated assessment tool,
when used in combination and in concert, can generate an
incredibly accurate profile of your personal strengths at this
moment in time. Take a moment to reflect upon the closing
words of the last sentence, for these words are of great importance and should not be overlooked. The words being "at this
moment in time." People will many times look at strengths as
a set group of behaviors that stay fixed over time, which in
many instances is true, but what is also true, and is also regu-
larly overlooked, is that new strengths can be cultivated if
there is desire, intent, time, and focused application toward
the desired new strength. The wisdom contained within this
truth is paramount to the process of personal growth and the
ongoing evolution of who we are as people.

Before closing this section, we need to make one final

connection and understanding regarding your personal and professional strengths that will segue the content into the next exploration and discovery area.

The renowned biographer Walter Isaacson's book *Steve Jobs* provides an amazingly intimate journey into the life and work of Steve Jobs. Isaacson's study of Jobs took place over two years and encompassed over 40 separate personal interviews with Jobs, as well as over 100 additional interviews with Jobs' family, friends, colleagues, and, dare I say, some borderline adversaries.[11] Isaacson's exploration into one of the world's most prominent figures (even in his death) and world-changing innovators was a journey of duplicity, to say the least. As Isaacson explored the man, the myth, and the legend that was Jobs, he found a man of strong views, insights, and convictions that, on many occasions, appeared (at least on the surface) to be in near contradiction to one another. For instance, and in perfect connection to the topic at hand, Steve Jobs has been cited with many memorable quotes. One that is tremendously saliant to the topic of self-knowledge and eventual authenticity, is as follows:

> *In most cases, strengths and weaknesses are two sides of the same coin. A strength in one situation is a weakness in another, yet often, the person can't switch gears. It's a very subtle thing to talk about strengths and weaknesses because, almost always, they're the same thing.*

Jobs' quote is a profound and deeply insightful statement that can easily be lost due to the duplicity of its context. The

surface meaning would appear to infer that the counter opposite of a strength is obviously a subsequent weakness. (Makes
sense.) But Jobs doesn't stop there. The last line of his quote
states that they are (in his opinion) one and the same. But how?
Candidly, we do not have a direct answer to this question, but
upon review and deeper reflection of the specific words that
Jobs used, it is plausible to infer that what is occurring is not
as much about the dichotomy of the words and concepts as it
is about the missed connections to whatever the targeted
behavior happens to be. Meaning that a *weakness* may simply
be an unaddressed or dormant potential strength that is
currently confined to some hidden space and not within our
current line of sight. A thin line between a strength and a weakness, like the edge of a coin, or in other words, a *blind spot*.

YOUR BLIND SPOTS

In 2003, the Swedish automobile maker Volvo became
the first commercial car company in the world to include a
system to detect blind spots while driving.[12] This system,
called the Blind Spot Information System or BLIS, is
designed to assist drivers and improve their awareness and
visibility while driving and, in turn, create a safer and more
secure driving experience.[13] Imagine if we too had a BLIS—
something (or someone) to help us survey our blind spots and
assist us in becoming more aware and more informed in the
process, allowing us to traverse the landscape of our lives
successfully. This will be the focus and the outcome of this
section of the chapter. However, first, there is still a bit more

to be learned from blind spot detection systems, how they work, and how they can be a model for us as individuals.

A group of researchers from the University of Alcalá in Madrid, Spain, produced a 2007 research paper entitled "Vision-Based Blind Spot Detection Using Optical Flow." The paper details how vision-based systems (cameras) are used for blind spot detection. The entire process of this technology begins with the obvious and most important first task—detection. This detection process is supported by a series of measures in which the cameras gather data. The computer system then completes a series of analyses involving the grouping and clustering of images, and from this data, a determination is made if there is something there (i.e., another vehicle).[14] If the system does indeed detect another vehicle, a complementary computer system engages, and a warning signal is activated that alerts the driver to take correction action and elude the unseen vehicle, or in the more recent model years, even takes control of the car and adjusts the path of the car without the guidance of the driver. The beauty of this system and process is that it gathers data, looks for patterns, and makes a final determination that will enhance the driver's ability to drive safely. This same process may be used by you, along with the assistance of your trusted confidants, as you determine what is currently residing within your own respective blind spots. Utilizing the same process of data gathering, pattern recognition, analysis of the findings, and feedback from others, you too may make decisions that will allow you to safely navigate life's challenges and be successful due to the recognition of personal behaviors, actions, or unseen strengths or hazards presently hidden from your current line of sight.

Researchers Kathryn Bollich, Paul Johannet, and Simine Vazire, in their article "In Search of Our True Selves: Feedback as a Path to Self-Knowledge," state that "the first step to improving self-knowledge is acknowledging one's blind spots." They go on to say that "the search for self-knowledge likely requires the active involvement of close others to help fill in our blind spots."[15] These findings support the work that you've done thus far, as well as provide credence to the power of exploring your respective blind spots as a means to further enlightenment. In essence, creating your own *human BLIS* as a way and means to learn about and utilize the insights gained through observation, self-reflection, and the assistance and feedback of others are the exact same processes that will be utilized in the next series of explorations.

Utilize the chart from Figure 1.1 or Exercise 1.4 and the space that follows, in conjunction with *The 3-Words Method*, to answer and chart your initial responses to the following two questions.

3-WORDS: **SELF**

- What three words best describe your top three suspected **PERSONAL BLIND SPOTS**?

    1. _____

    2. _____

    3. _____

- What three words best describe your top three suspected **PROFESSIONAL BLIND SPOTS**?

    1. _____

    2. _____

    3. _____

Exercise 1.4

With these initial introspective blind spots tasks now completed, once again enlist a cross-section of family members, close friends, colleagues, and confidants to provide you with their insights and then chart their responses to the following questions. But before you ask each individual the questions that follow, it may be wise to give them some context as to the term *blind spot*, being that they will not have been privy to the context just described.

It is recommended that you present the idea of a blind spot as follows: "A blind spot is an unseen, yet still present, challenge, short-coming, or attribute. In the case of shortcomings or less flattering attributes, these are characteristics, behaviors, or actions that may be a hindrance to me and my personal or professional growth. And on the flip side, what other attributes do you see in me (that I may not) that are, in your opinion, unaddressed or dormant potential strengths yet to be discovered or developed by me and have the potential to be used for greater personal and professional growth in the future?" Capture the insights from others in Exercise 1.5.

3-WORDS: **OTHERS**

- In your opinion, what three words best describe my top three **PERSONAL BLIND SPOTS**?

1. _____	1. _____	1. _____
2. _____	2. _____	2. _____
3. _____	3. _____	3. _____
Name:_____	Name:_____	Name:_____

- In your opinion, what three words best describe my top three **PROFESSIONAL BLIND SPOTS**?

1. _____	1. _____	1. _____
2. _____	2. _____	2. _____
3. _____	3. _____	3. _____
Name:_____	Name:_____	Name:_____

Exercise 1.5

(Optional activity with an additional cost associated) Utilizing the full list of all 34 strengths from the Strengths-Finder 2.0 assessment, focus on the bottom third (numbers 23-34) and review and report the findings below.

 ONLINE RESOURCE: STRENGTHS 23-24

23. _____   27. _____   31. _____

24. _____   28. _____   32. _____

25. _____   29. _____   33. _____

26. _____   30. _____   34. _____

Exercise 1.6 (Optional)

Considering the totality of your collected blind spots data to this point, including your personally generated list of potential blind spots, the lists of words and feedback gained from your family, friends, colleagues, and confidants through the use of *The 3-Words Method*, as well as your results from the purchased assessment (if this resource was utilized), now take some time to carefully look at and review each piece of data. Utilizing Tool 3 from the onset of this chapter, pause and reflect on the totality of the data collected and what it says about you. While doing so, remember to grant yourself the permission of time to *dig deep*, and conduct some deep reflection while also using the concession of *grace* while you review and answer the following questions in Reflection 1.2.

 **REFLECTION**

1. What's resonating with you, or landing on you, based upon the collected data and your respective results?

_____

_____

_____

_____

_____

2. Were there any surprises? If so, what were they?

_____

_____

_____

_____

_____

3. What will you do with either the affirmations or unexpected insights gained through these exercises?

_____

_____

_____

_____

_____

Reflection 1.2

With the insights and feedback regarding your respective blind spots in hand, you are more than likely still reflecting, processing, and even wrangling with what these new insights have brought to light. If this is the case, that's fine. It's important to remember that personal and professional growth is a journey, and with any journey, there will be struggles. These struggles are not only typical but are necessary to allow growth to occur and are vital to your journey.

With that said, the results of each of the exercises you have just completed may have felt somewhat uncomfortable and possibly even painful to receive or acknowledge. But again, this insight is essential for growth and is a fundamental part of the discovery process.

Don Hamachek, former professor of counseling and educational psychology at Michigan State University, brings this portion of your discovery process into focus with this statement: "Knowing oneself, deeply and fully, involves facing oneself, squarely and honestly."[16] This "facing oneself, squarely and honestly," is one of the most challenging yet crucial tasks in personal growth. Identifying and accepting the aspects of oneself that are not so flattering or that one struggles with, as well as those that are completely unknown can be daunting. The circumstance or manner in which you have become enlightened to these respective blind spots does not matter. What does matter is that they are no longer in that unseen, undetectable void and can be addressed or explored further. And, in doing so, you can then safely "switch lanes" and know that you will not only be safe, but will also arrive at your destination better off than when you originally departed—just like the drivers of all those Volvos.

YOUR CONTRIBUTIONS

Arthur M. Schlesinger, Sr., renowned author, American historian, and Harvard professor, authored an article for *The Atlantic* entitled "Our Ten Contributions to Civilization." As the title proclaims, Schlesinger details ten specific contributions that the United States of America has championed and given to human civilization as a whole and for its betterment.

The article begins with Schlesinger citing the Declaration of Independence and the doctrine that:

> *...all men are created equal, that they are endowed by their Creator with certain unalienable Rights, that among these are Life, Liberty and the pursuit of Happiness.*

Schlesinger states that this is the starting point—the right to revolt against tyranny and vie for one's independence. From this inception, we (the United States) have espoused the Principle of Federalism, that is, smaller, self-governing units that collectively constitute an entity larger than its units. This Federalist Principle and stance has helped others to birth their own collective, such as the first League of Nations and the United Nations. The next contribution is what he calls "The Consent of the Governed," meaning the throwing off of the ideas centered on and around monarchies, nobility, or hereditary governance and instead being a "government of the people, by the people, and for the people." From these three foundational tenets, we as a country (as a union) have championed and elevated women and women's rights, welcomed and fused together immigrants from around the world into one "single society," championed freedom of religion, required free and appropriate public education for all children, established the construct of voluntary giving for altruistic purposes (i.e., giving to schools, churches, missions, charities, etc.), created technologies that have transformed the country and the world, and lastly, what Schlesinger called "Evolutionary Progress." While citing Abraham Lincoln, he concludes that Americans ascribe to the simple belief that "the legitimate object of government is to do for a community of people whatever they need to have done but cannot do at all, or cannot do so well, for themselves, in their separate and individual capacities." When you pause and reflect upon what Schlesinger has outlined, these contributions are truly remarkable in themselves, but collectively constitute a model for not only modern civilization but also future civilizations. A construct for an ideal world based upon a unified, uplifted, and functional civilization for all.[17]

This idea of contributions to and for the greater good and simultaneously having an enduring value in the process is paramount and timeless, much like Schlesinger's article, which was written for the March issue of *The Atlantic* in 1959. The idea that we, as a collective, as a country, and as a form of government, have much to offer this world is one thing, but how does that translate to you as an individual? The concept of you *paying it forward* and contributing to others and the world at large for the greater good of all sounds wonderful, yet just a bit grandiose. Or does it? The real question here is, *what constitutes your world*? What does your world look like?

Is your world comprised of your family and loved ones? Close friends and colleagues? Business associates and clients? Or a combination of all of the above? If so, and even if not viewed as such in your own mind, it still is the world in which you live and interact on an all but daily basis. Meaning, you're engaging with and impacting your world each day. And as you're doing so, you're likely doing it without any desire for recognition. Begging the question, *what do you have to offer to others and the world*? What are *your* specific contributions? And how will these contributions enrich and improve your and others' lives? This will be the next exploration.

Thus far, you have explored your areas of strengths and just concluded uncovering your respective blind spots, which now leads to uncovering your individual contributions. Contributions are the things that you have to offer to your immediate world and, even potentially, the world at large. This portion of your exploration and journey will be a little more challenging to identify and name, especially if you're still in the early stages of self-discovery, because your awareness of your respective contributions may not be immediately identified or known. For example, a middle school teacher quietly makes a profound impact on one of their students, and this impact is not exposed (or brought to light) until a chance meeting in the distant future. At this chance meeting, the former student, now an adult, confides to their former teacher the profound impact they have had on their life and how their time together changed the course of their life forever! A revelation of the impact the teacher made is only now being offered up many, many years in the future, and at the intersection of a chance encounter. As the example shows, you may not know the impact of your contributions until some future date. Hopefully, that will not always be the case, and your respective contributions will be made in the here and now.

Researchers Simine Vazire and Erika N. Carlson, in their journal publication "Others Sometimes Know Us Better Than We Know Ourselves," provide credence to the need for this type of trusted partnership to help us gain a more "complete picture" of ourselves in our quest for discovery and true self-knowledge. The need for these trusted alliances is partly due to several key assertions from their research. One of the first assertions is that when we are on a journey toward self-knowledge, we tend to, citing Vazire and Carlson, "ignore aspects of our personality that others can detect." More specifically, and again citing the researchers, "many aspects of personality are remarkably transparent to others, even when we are not intentionally broadcasting them."[18] This means that others very often do know us better than we know ourselves. But how? We (more than anyone else) should know and understand ourselves best. But herein lies the rub. When we look inward, we tend to, but not always, view ourselves through lenses that are, at best, "distorted." This distortion is yet another reason for enlisting the assistance of others to help us overcome this simple human flaw. Flaws that allow our appraisals to be grounded in our *desired way of being* as opposed to our *actual demonstration* or self-assessments that may even be partnered with unintentional or intentional biases. These factors give credence to the need for fellow guides along the way, helping us to gain a truer picture of what we have to offer. If none of these are true for you, please know that every one of us has been guilty at one time or another of being unable to adequately assess our abilities, especially when it comes to identifying and naming our respective contributions.

The need for trustworthy partners on your journey of discovery has been strongly suggested to this point. It is especially so now, as it pertains to identifying contributions to others and the world. To that point, there are some factors to consider when contemplating and selecting *contributions partners* to assist you along this journey. The partner guides that you select should be individuals who know you well and should be able to meet the following three criteria:

CRITERIA 1: **CONNECTION**

Your connection with and to the individual is relatively strong, meaning you can openly share a variety of topics and content without judgment.

CRITERIA 2: **TIME**

There is some longevity in the relationship with your contributions partner, and the amount and frequency of time spent with the individual are relatively high and consistent.

CRITERIA 3: **CANDOR**

You have been open and honest with this individual, demonstrating your "true self" to them in various settings and circumstances.

These three criteria should guide you well and give you a good basis for determining who your *contributions partners* should and will be. With this determined, and once again utilizing the chart from Figure 1.1 or Exercise 1.7 and the space that follows, in conjunction with *The 3-Words Method*, you should answer and chart your initial responses to the following two questions.

 ## 3-WORDS: **SELF**

- What three words best describe your **PERSONAL CONTRIBUTIONS** to this life and the world?

    1. _____

    2. _____

    3. _____

- What three words best describe your **PROFESSIONAL CONTRIBUTIONS** to this life and the world?

    1. _____

    2. _____

    3. _____

Exercise 1.7

Utilizing the chart from Figure 1.1 or Exercise 1.8, and in the following space in conjunction with *The 3-Words Method* and a cross-section of family, friends, colleagues, and confidants, answer and chart their responses to the following questions.

 3-WORDS: **OTHERS**

- In your opinion, what three words best describe my top three **PERSONAL CONTRIBUTIONS** to this life and the world?

1. _____	1. _____	1. _____
2. _____	2. _____	2. _____
3. _____	3. _____	3. _____
Name:_____	Name:_____	Name:_____

- In your opinion, what three words best describe my top three **PROFESSIONAL CONTRIBUTIONS** to this life and the world?

1. _____	1. _____	1. _____
2. _____	2. _____	2. _____
3. _____	3. _____	3. _____
Name:_____	Name:_____	Name:_____

Exercise 1.8

Utilizing the *3-Words* given to you by your personal and professional contributions partners, ask them to now explain each of the words given to you and why they chose them. In addition, ask them to share the insights and context that led them to select these words for you, along with examples of how your demonstrated contributions are being received, used, and enriching others. Capture these responses and insights in Exercise 1.9.

DIGGING DEEPER
PERSONAL CONTRIBUTION

PERSONAL CONTRIBUTION PARTNER **1**

Word 1 _____ : _____

_____

_____

Word 2 _____ : _____

_____

_____

Word 3 _____ : _____

_____

_____

PERSONAL CONTRIBUTION PARTNER **2**

Word 1 _____ : _____

_____

_____

Word 2 _____ : _____

_____

_____

Word 3 _____ : _____

_____

_____

PERSONAL CONTRIBUTION PARTNER **3**

Word 1 _____ : _____
_____
_____

Word 2 _____ : _____
_____
_____

Word 3 _____ : _____
_____
_____

Exercise 1.9a (In conjunction with Exercise 1.8 above)

⊕ DIGGING DEEPER
PROFESSIONAL CONTRIBUTION

PROFESSIONAL CONTRIBUTION PARTNER **1**

Word 1 _____ : _____
_____
_____

Word 2 _____ : _____
_____
_____

Word 3 _____ : _____
_____
_____

PROFESSIONAL CONTRIBUTION PARTNER **2**

Word 1 _____ : _____

_____

_____

Word 2 _____ : _____

_____

_____

Word 3 _____ : _____

_____

_____

PROFESSIONAL CONTRIBUTION PARTNER **3**

Word 1 _____ : _____

_____

_____

Word 2 _____ : _____

_____

_____

Word 3 _____ : _____

_____

_____

Exercise 1.9b (In conjunction with Exercise 1.8 above)

At this time, review your personally generated list of contributions, the lists of words, and feedback gained from your family, friends, colleagues, and confidants through the use of *The 3-Words Method* and the additional insights gathered in Exercises 1.8 and 1.9. Take each insight and utilizing

Tool 3 from the onset of this chapter once again, pause and reflect on the totality of the data collected, and what it says about you. While doing so, remember to grant yourself the permission of time to *dig deep* and the concession of *grace* while you review and answer the following questions in Reflection 1.3.

 **REFLECTION**

1. What's resonating with you, or landing on you, based upon the collected data and your respective results?

_____

_____

_____

_____

_____

2. Were there any surprises? If so, what were they?

_____

_____

_____

_____

_____

3. What will you do with either the affirmations or unexpected insights gained through these exercises?

_____

_____

_____

_____

_____

Reflection 1.3

If you are feeling somewhat uninspired by your contributions, realize that no matter the size of the contribution, it is still, nonetheless, a contribution. In addition, remember that your journey is really just beginning. You have an entire life ahead of you to utilize all that you are learning about yourself and develop and gift even more of yourself going forward. If this last fact is still not enough, consider the words of Nelson Mandela, Nobel Peace Prize recipient, former president of South Africa, and one of the great thinkers, activists, and leaders of the twentieth century who shared the following thoughts during a 2005 interview, He stated that "there are so many men and women who hold no distinctive positions but whose contribution towards the development of society has been enormous."[19] Take a moment to think about that statement. Your contributions to the world can be great, or they can be small, but whatever your viewpoint, never lose sight of the fact that more often than not, and more often than you realize or give yourself credit for, the smallest contributions are typically the ones that in the end are indeed the greatest of them all. As the full title of Malcolm Gladwell's wonderful book *The Tipping Point: How Little Things Can Make a Big Difference* suggests, it is many times the little things in life that make the biggest difference.[20] A difference in how your gifts and contributions are passed on and are paid forward, much like the middle school teacher to their student those many years prior and how the power of their contribution did indeed make a difference.

PART 1: SELF-KNOWLEDGE
IN SUMMARY

Who are you? Three words; one question. A question whose answer is greater than the sum of its parts. In answering this question, you gain knowledge and insight into who you are. This knowledge—this self-knowledge—enlightens you to the core aspects of you. This enlightenment is accomplished by looking inward, and by means of enlisting the help of other trusted individuals to help you realize and become the next best version of yourself. This discovery, realization, and acknowledgment is gained through appraisals of your strengths, blind spots, and contributions.

You begin enlightenment by gaining access to your respective areas of strengths—the things that you do well. Strengths are powerful forces in your life and provide you with much of the confidence that drives you forward. In recognizing these strengths, you learn how to elevate yourself (and others) even further and can do so with the confidence that comes from acknowledging these strengths. But not all strengths are obvious or seen at first sight. Some may be hidden in places you cannot see or are just simply blind to.

Blind spots are challenging places. They can house behaviors and attributes that impact you in ways you may not even know. The size and power of these blind spots may keep you from succeeding. The aspects that reside in this "unseen area" may be hindering your personal and professional growth and progress. Even though potentially unseen by you, others can detect these aspects of you and help you navigate in and around these blind spots—especially if the attribute you do not see is an unrecognized or dormant potential future strength that is just waiting to be discovered. Or better yet, a contribution that the world is just waiting to receive.

You have much to contribute to this life and this world. Your world can be large, or it can be small; it doesn't really matter. What matters is that you are contributing to that world and that your contributions are impacting those around you. Those around you are the recipients of the actions that you are "paying forward" for the betterment of them and those around them. Contributions are also powerful forces in this life and can change the lives of others in profound ways—ways you may never even know about. But that is okay. Contributions are the gifts you give, and if you are truly altruistic, you need not receive anything in return other than the satisfaction gained from contributing positively to someone else's life.

SO NOW WHAT?
(ACTION STEPS)

ACTION STEP 1: **YOUR STRENGTHS**

Lean into your strengths as much and as often as possible.
Strive to make your identified strengths even stronger.

ACTION STEP 2: **YOUR BLIND SPOTS**

Leverage your blind spots for what they are: an opportunity
to discover and make seen (or better) something that may have
always been there but may simply have been out of sight.

ACTION STEP 3: **YOUR CONTRIBUTIONS**

Gift your contributions to the world. Gifting these parts of
yourself to others is one of the most personally fulfilling
endeavors in life and an excellent pathway to authenticity.

SELF: PART 2

KNOW HOW & WHY YOU ARE:
THE POWER OF SELF-CONCEPT

"The curious paradox is that when I accept myself just as I am, then I can change."
- Carl Rogers

In 1981, researchers Dr. Russell Fazio, Edwin Effrein, and Victoria Falender from Indiana University published an article in the *Journal of Personality and Social Psychology* entitled "Self-Perceptions Following Social Interaction." In their article, they detailed their findings regarding a recent social experiment that they had conducted. In this experiment, the researchers sought to initiate and verify recent psychological research and insights pertaining to, in their words, "the links between social perception and social interaction." In the study, the researchers strived to find out and corroborate how we can project, many times unknowingly, our beliefs and expectations about another person to such an extent that the other person will not only match our expectations at that moment but will continue the behavior in the same manner in follow up interactions, even if the demonstrated behavior is not typically how that person would normally act.[21]

Looking at it another way, Person A and Person B are about to meet. Before the meeting, Person A assumes how Person B will act and behave. The two then meet. At this initial meeting, Person A begins to subconsciously project and speak, as well as act in a manner that will, in their mind, align with how they believe that Person B will present and behave. Once this happens, this unconscious projection and the verbal interaction by Person A to Person B will cause Person B to begin to behave in a way that will affirm Person A's belief—even if Person B would normally never act that way. As the researchers describe it, this new, *atypical* behavior by Person B creates a "self-fulfilling prophecy." Even more interesting than that, Person B will continue to behave in the same manner in all future interactions with Person A, as well as with others beyond Person A and in other social interactions, even if this is not their *true* behavior. Amazing!

How and why does this phenomenon occur? Fazio and

his colleagues note that once an individual, our Person B, behaves a certain way, they may go through a "self-perception process and internalize the very disposition that the perceiver [our Person A] expected him or her to possess." In short, Person B will start to become that *expectation* and will then begin to experience a "change in…self-concept." A *change* that will not only affect their behavior with and toward Person A in the future but will also "affect his or her behavior in future and different situations not involving the original perceiver [Person A]." What the researchers found is that we can and do change who we are (our self-concept) and how we present ourselves to the world based upon the subconscious projections, verbal interactions, and even the biases of other people. We then internalize this "false behavior" while carrying that behavior forward into other aspects of our daily lives and in different contexts and circumstances. Again, amazing! Terrifying, but nonetheless amazing!

To understand this behavioral transformation more fully, as well as how you will be able to use this knowledge going forward, and within your journey of discovery, we will do the following:

1. Take a closer look at the experiment itself.

2. Revisit the researchers' findings.

3. Utilize these new insights as a guide for moving forward.

THE EXPERIMENT: **A CLOSER LOOK**

The study began with the researchers enlisting the assistance of forty-two students as participants in an experiment as a portion of the requirement for the completion of an introductory psychology course. At the onset of the study, the students were only told that the experiment would involve "Personality Interviewing." The first stage of the experiment involved each student being individually met by a member of the research team. At this initial meeting, the researcher would casually talk about the various psychology courses offered at the university, and all-the-while they would be conducting an initial assessment of the student and their level of introversion (staying to oneself) or extroversion (outgoing and sociable). Specifically, they would rate the students on a scale of -3 to +3, where the lower end was assigned a label of "very introverted" and the opposite end was "very extroverted." From this initial assessment, the researcher then assigned each student, without the students' knowledge of their respective assessment score, to one of two groups: The Introvert Group or The Extrovert Group.

After this initial exchange between the researcher and the student, the student was led to an "experimental room." Once in the room, the researcher presented information and research pertaining to the experiment topic of "personality interviewing" and explained that they "would be asked to respond verbally to a set of interview questions," which were to be recorded for the first portion of the experiment, and then following this task, they would be asked to listen to recordings of other participants and rate them based upon certain "personality trait dimensions." With the instructions completed and the steps and expectations understood, the researcher proceeded to provide the student with a stack of ten index cards.

Each of the ten cards contained a single question that they were to read silently and then respond to verbally, at which time their answers were recorded. The questions posed to the students were taken from a list generated by two fellow researchers, Mark Snyder and William Swann, from the University of Minnesota, during similar experiments and studies they had conducted several years prior.[22] Of the ten questions, two of the questions were deemed to be "neutral in nature," meaning, for instance, "What are your career goals?" and "What are some of your favorite books?" The remaining eight questions were each constructed in such a way that they intended to manipulate the student toward one of two opposing slants, either introverted or extroverted conditions. For instance, the questions slanted toward the introvert condition were in the realm and context of "What things do you dislike about loud parties?"

Conversely, the questions that were slanted toward the extrovert condition were in the realm and context of "What would you do if you wanted to liven things up at a party?" Once all questions were read, answered, and recorded, thus ending the first portion of the experiment, the student was then ushered to another larger room within the research laboratory by the researcher. As the researcher and the student arrived at the laboratory room door, the researcher informed the student that they needed to run to another room downstairs to gather the recording that the student would need to listen to and evaluate as part of the second portion of the experiment. With the announcement of this misstep, the researcher then asks the student to "have a seat" in the adjoining waiting room. As they enter the waiting room, a folding chair is closed and leaning against the outside wall and just to the right of the doorway. At this moment, the researcher remarks, "If you could grab that chair there and sit in the waiting room, I'll come back shortly, and we can listen to the tape. Thanks." The researcher then leaves the room and does not return for ten minutes.

Once the researcher left the room, and unbeknownst to the student subject, the next piece of data was gathered via the students' actions. In the far corner of the waiting room sat another student (presumedly waiting for their turn in the experiment), who was in fact part of the experiment and was a conspirator with the researchers. The conspirator was a fellow student (female) who was seated with her purse set on the chair next to her, which also contained a recording device. The conspirator was sitting quietly and reading a copy of the university newspaper. The student conspirator knew nothing about the experiment process, except that "she was not allowed to initiate conversation when the subject entered the room" and during the 10-minute waiting period.

After the researcher returned to the room and retrieved the other student, the conspirator researcher was to document the data collected on their fellow student. This data included "whether the subject [student] had initiated a conversation," as well as recording the total number of floor tiles (blocks) that were "between the two nearest legs of the subject's [student's] chair and her own chair." The conspirator researcher was then required to rate the student subject on the same introvert/extrovert scale initially used by the primary researcher of -3 (very introverted) to +3 (very extroverted). In addition to the rating scale, the conspirator was asked to indicate if she believed the student subject was acting in an introverted or extroverted manner during their time in the room or if they could not adequately assess this based upon their observation.

Lastly, once the student subject had reached the other laboratory room, the students were asked to complete a "trait inventory" of themselves, similar to the one used by Snyder and Swann in their corollary research. The inventory consisted of 10 questions that were on a 6-point Likert scale (e.g., very X, X, somewhat X, somewhat Y, Y, very Y) for the traits of: "talkative/quiet; unsociable/sociable; friendly/unfriendly; poised/awkward; extroverted/introverted; enthusiastic/apathetic; outgoing/shy; energetic/relaxed; warm/cold; confident/unconfident." After all of the data elements were completed and gathered, the researcher interviewed and debriefed each of the student subjects, thereby ending the experiment.

THE EXPERIMENT: **THE FINDINGS**

After the overall experiment was concluded, the collected and analyzed data revealed some notable findings and results. The main finding came by means of the student (female) conspirator located in the waiting room and her observations and ratings after her interactions with the student subject in the waiting room. Following her 10-minute interaction with each student subject, she accurately categorized 26 out of the 37 (or 70%) of the student subjects as exhibiting either introverted or extroverted tendencies. This was supported by the fact that 75% of the students who had been conditioned to be "extroverted" initiated conversation with the female conspirator and tended to sit closer to the conspirator than their introvert counterparts. The student subjects who had been conditioned to be "introverted" only initiated conversation 50% of the time and tended to position their chairs so that they were seated farther away from the female conspirator. Fascinating!

NEW INSIGHTS: A GUIDE

The fact that people are potentially vulnerable to the projected thoughts and unfounded beliefs of another person is all the more reason why you need to take the time and allocate the energy to self-reflect.[23] This self-reflection process will allow you to gain personal insight into how and why you are the way you are (i.e., your self-concept).[24] Without a solid self-concept, you may fall prey to internalizing and then demonstrating an image of yourself that is not at all based on who you truly are, but simply *mimicking* what others believe about you and who you should be. On the contrary, a solid self-concept will allow you to confidently demonstrate your *true authentic self* through knowing how and why you think, process, and present your "true you" to the world.

HOW YOU THINK

In the mid-1980s, Dr. Anthony Gregorc, former professor at the University of Illinois at Urbana and the University of Connecticut, developed a model for categorizing and explaining how the mind works, and how this knowledge may then be used to understand how we think about and then process the world around us. His research, which he dubbed the *Mind Styles Model,* breaks the mind and cognitive processes into two distinct categories: *Perceptual Qualities* and *Ordering Abilities.* These two categories are then divided into two more clearly defined yet polar opposite subsets. The subset of the Perceptual Qualities being labeled as either *Concrete* or *Abstract*, and the subset of the Ordering Abilities being labeled as either *Sequential* or *Random*. With these qualities and abilities as his foundation, Gregorc then paired each subset trait, creating four distinct styles of mind. These *Mind/Thinking Styles* being - *Concrete Sequential, Concrete Random, Abstract Random,* and *Abstract Sequential.*[25] To understand the model and each style more fully, I have taken Gregorc's construct and defined each of the four style types in more people-oriented terms. The terms and definitions are summarized as follows and may be found in Figure 2.1.

CONCRETE SEQUENTIAL

This individual is solidly based in reality and thinks about and sees the world in a very logical, subsequent, and orderly manner.

CONCRETE RANDOM

This individual, while still being based in reality, also has the capability for visionary thinking and is willing to experiment with ideas to allow their vision to come to fruition.

ABSTRACT RANDOM

This individual thrives in unstructured and undefined (people-oriented) environments where non-linear thinking is the norm.

ABSTRACT SEQUENTIAL

While still embracing many of the benefits of flexible environments, this individual also gravitates toward theory, data, and analysis.

MIND/THINKING STYLES MODEL - SUMMARY

Mind/Thinking Styles Model			The Power of *Self*
Concrete Sequential	**Concrete Random**	**Abstract Random**	**Abstract Sequential**
PERCEPTUAL QUALITIES This individual is solidly based in reality and thinks about and sees the world	This individual, while still being based in reality, also has the	This individual thrives in unstructured and undefined (people-oriented) environments	While still embracing many of the benefits of flexible environments, this individual
ORDERING ABILITIES in a very logical, subsequent, and orderly manner.	capability for visionary thinking and is willing to experiment with ideas to allow their vision to come to fruition.	where non-linear thinking is the norm.	also gravitates toward theory, data, and analysis.

Adapted by Dr. Keith Floyd from Dr. Anthony Gregorc's Mind Styles Model

Figure 2.1

These four mind/thinking styles provide a context, an identification process, and a categorization model for how you look at, think about, and process the world around you. How you think influences and controls much of what you do in life. To that end, it is all the more reason to find out how you receive, process, and function within the world based upon how you think and how this thinking guides you. To identify and categorize your respective thinking style, you will need to complete the *Mind/Thinking Styles Assessment* found in Exercise 2.1.

MIND/THINKING STYLES
ASSESSMENT & TOOLS

Utilizing Figures 2.2 through 2.4 or the downloaded PDF versions of the assessment and tools from *The Power of Self* book website (www.ThePowerofSelfbook.com), complete the following tasks:

TASK # 1

Self-administer the *Mind/Thinking Styles Assessment* (Figure 2.2) per the instructions on the assessment.

TASK # 2

Transfer your responses from your *Mind/Thinking Styles Assessment* (Figure 2.2) to the *Mind/Thinking Styles Assessment: Answer Key* (Figure 2.3) by means of assigning your answer selections to the corresponding Group A (Concrete or Sequential) or Group B (Abstract or Random) designations on the answer key.

TASK # 3

Transfer your designations from the *Mind/Thinking Styles Assessment: Answer Key* (Figure 2.3) to the *Mind/Thinking Styles Assessment: Scoring Guide* (Figure 2.4) and follow the scoring instructions to determine your specific mind/thinking style.

Note: If any of your score totals ends in a tie, choose the Quality (Concrete or Abstract) or Ability (Sequential or Random) you tend to default to when you are presented with a challenging situation.

Exercise 2.1

MIND/THINKING STYLES - ASSESSMENT

Mind/Thinking Styles Model   The Power of *Self*

| Concrete Sequential | Concrete Random | Abstract Random | Abstract Sequential |

ASSESSMENT

INSTRUCTIONS:

READ EACH PAIR OF WORDS AND CHECK THE BOX NEXT TO THE WORD THAT RESONATES WITH YOU THE MOST

	GROUP A	GROUP B
1.	PARTICULAR	FLEXIBLE
2.	METHODICAL	HAPHAZARD
3.	PRECISE	GENERAL
4.	METICULOUS	ARBITRARY
5.	DETAILED	RELAXED
6.	SYSTEMATIC	INCIDENTAL
7.	SPECIFIC	ABSTRACT
8.	PLANNED	SPONTANEOUS
9.	CONNECTED	DISJOINTED
10.	ROUTINE	CHANGEABLE
11.	TANGIBLE	HYPOTHETICAL
12.	PERSISTENT	INTERMITTENT
13.	SUBSTANTIAL	PHILOSOPHICAL
14.	PURPOSEFUL	HAPPENSTANCE
15.	STEADY	LOOSE
16.	ACCURATE	RANDOM
17.	ORDERLY	NONCONCRETE
18.	DEFINITE	COINCIDENTAL
19.	CONSTANT	FREE
20.	SOLID	WONDERING

Developed by: Dr. Keith Floyd based upon Dr. Anthony Gregorc's Mind Styles Model

Figure 2.2

MIND/THINKING STYLES - ASSESSMENT
ANSWER KEY

Mind/Thinking Styles Model   The Power of *Self*

| Concrete Sequential | Concrete Random | Abstract Random | Abstract Sequential |

ASSESSMENT: **ANSWER KEY**

INSTRUCTIONS:

TRANSFER YOUR ANSWERS FROM YOUR ASSESSMENT TO THIS ANSWER KEY

	GROUP A		GROUP B
1.	☐ CONCRETE	☐	ABSTRACT
2.	☐ SEQUENTIAL	☐	RANDOM
3.	☐ CONCRETE	☐	ABSTRACT
4.	☐ SEQUENTIAL	☐	RANDOM
5.	☐ CONCRETE	☐	ABSTRACT
6.	☐ SEQUENTIAL	☐	RANDOM
7.	☐ CONCRETE	☐	ABSTRACT
8.	☐ SEQUENTIAL	☐	RANDOM
9.	☐ CONCRETE	☐	ABSTRACT
10.	☐ SEQUENTIAL	☐	RANDOM
11.	☐ CONCRETE	☐	ABSTRACT
12.	☐ SEQUENTIAL	☐	RANDOM
13.	☐ CONCRETE	☐	ABSTRACT
14.	☐ SEQUENTIAL	☐	RANDOM
15.	☐ SEQUENTIAL	☐	ABSTRACT
16.	☐ CONCRETE	☐	RANDOM
17.	☐ SEQUENTIAL	☐	ABSTRACT
18.	☐ CONCRETE	☐	RANDOM
19.	☐ SEQUENTIAL	☐	ABSTRACT
20.	☐ CONCRETE	☐	RANDOM

Developed by: Dr. Keith Floyd based upon Dr. Anthony Gregorc's Mind Styles Model

Figure 2.3

MIND/THINKING STYLES - ASSESSMENT
SCORING GUIDE

Mind/Thinking Styles Model   The Power of *Self*

Concrete Sequential	Concrete Random	Abstract Random	Abstract Sequential

ASSESSMENT: **SCORING GUIDE**

INSTRUCTIONS:

TRANSFER YOUR PERCEPTUAL & ORDERING RESPONSES TO THIS SCORING GUIDE, THEN TOTAL EACH QUALITY OR ABILITY.
THE HIGHEST NUMBER OUT OF YOUR PERCEPTUAL & ORDERING CATEGORIES WILL PROVIDE YOU WITH YOUR RESPECTIVE MIND/THINKING STYLE.*
(* NOTE: IF YOU END IN A TIE, CHOOSE THE QUALITY OR ABILITY THAT YOU TEND TO DEFAULT TO WHEN YOU ARE PRESENTED WITH A CHALLENGING SITUATION)

	GROUP A			GROUP B	
1.	CONCRETE	SEQUENTIAL	ABSTRACT	RANDOM
2.	CONCRETE	SEQUENTIAL	ABSTRACT	RANDOM
3.	CONCRETE	SEQUENTIAL	ABSTRACT	RANDOM
4.	CONCRETE	SEQUENTIAL	ABSTRACT	RANDOM
5.	CONCRETE	SEQUENTIAL	ABSTRACT	RANDOM
6.	CONCRETE	SEQUENTIAL	ABSTRACT	RANDOM
7.	CONCRETE	SEQUENTIAL	ABSTRACT	RANDOM
8.	CONCRETE	SEQUENTIAL	ABSTRACT	RANDOM
9.	CONCRETE	SEQUENTIAL	ABSTRACT	RANDOM
10.	CONCRETE	SEQUENTIAL	ABSTRACT	RANDOM
11.	CONCRETE	SEQUENTIAL	ABSTRACT	RANDOM
12.	CONCRETE	SEQUENTIAL	ABSTRACT	RANDOM
13.	CONCRETE	SEQUENTIAL	ABSTRACT	RANDOM
14.	CONCRETE	SEQUENTIAL	ABSTRACT	RANDOM
15.	CONCRETE	SEQUENTIAL	ABSTRACT	RANDOM
16.	CONCRETE	SEQUENTIAL	ABSTRACT	RANDOM
17.	CONCRETE	SEQUENTIAL	ABSTRACT	RANDOM
18.	CONCRETE	SEQUENTIAL	ABSTRACT	RANDOM
19.	CONCRETE	SEQUENTIAL	ABSTRACT	RANDOM
20.	CONCRETE	SEQUENTIAL	ABSTRACT	RANDOM

TOTALS: _____ X 5 = _____ | _____ X 5 = _____ | _____ X 5 = _____ | _____ X 5 = _____

PERCEPTUAL QUALITY: _____   **ORDERING** ABILITY: _____
(CONCRETE OR ABSTRACT)   (SEQUENTIAL OR RANDOM)

Developed by: Dr. Keith Floyd based upon Dr. Anthony Gregorc's Mind Styles Model

Figure 2.4

With the *Mind/Thinking Styles Assessment* now completed, take a few moments to review your assessment results, and from the results and your findings, answer the following questions in Reflection 2.1.

 **REFLECTION**

1. Based on your assessment results, what's resonating with you or landing on you?

_____

_____

_____

_____

_____

2. Were there any surprises? If so, what were they?

_____

_____

_____

_____

_____

3. What will you do with either the affirmations or unexpected insights gained through these exercises?

_____

_____

_____

_____

_____

Reflection 2.1

The assessment tool you just utilized and the subsequent reflections are intended to give you insight and perspective into "how you think." An insight and perspective that may very well be a *first-of-its-kind* discovery for you. But this is only the first step, for *how* you think is merely the base upon which *why you think that way* is built.

WHY YOU THINK IT

Dr. Anthony Gregorc's research, work, and model are geared toward education and the tendencies of thinkers and learners. This slant toward learning, by means of the intersection of mind and thinking, is done so that the instruction being presented may be more focused and personalized to the learner and their individual needs. In doing so, the instructor creates the conditions necessary for optimizing student learning by fully engaging and connecting with the students, and they, in turn, with the content. This engagement is only possible by knowing how each learner receives, connects with, and processes the information. This understanding is paramount for instruction, learning, and in the context of this book, for the demonstration of your true self in an authentic manner by possessing a solid understanding of why you think a certain way and the role this type of thinking plays in your greater self-concept.

This quest for understanding will begin by breaking down each of the Mind/Thinking Styles more fully, allowing you to gain a greater mastery of your respective style. To accomplish this specific learning and allow for greater discernment, each style will be reviewed through the lenses of "Likes, Ideals, and Challenges." Once each style has been deconstructed and explained, you will be asked to complete a series of reflection activities for each of the styles—specifically exploring the style that you most closely align with via your *Mind/Thinking Styles Assessment* to gain even greater insight and understanding of yourself by way of how and why you think the way you do.

Concrete
Sequential

MIND/THINKING STYLE:
CONCRETE SEQUENTIAL

This individual is solidly based in reality and thinks about and sees the world in a very logical, subsequent, and orderly manner.

THIS THINKER:

 **LIKES:**

RULES – Rules are part of the control these types of thinkers like to have at their disposal. Rules give them context and a method to navigate their world.

SPECIFICS – Whereas rules assist with navigating their world, specifics allow their world to progress in an orderly fashion.

ORDER – This, of all of the Likes, is the one that typically allows the individual to function and thrive. When there is order, the world makes the most sense, and when there is no order, working and functioning within the world becomes extremely difficult.

FACTS – These are the keys to unlocking the world. This type of thinker doesn't need much more than the facts. Facts inform them, and facts guide them.

 **IDEALS:**

STRUCTURE – Structure gives this type of thinker parameters and a context in which to live and work.

ROUTINES – These are the lifeblood of the Concrete Sequential thinker. Routines coincide with their affinity for order and allow this type of thinker to progress through each day with a purpose and a plan.

PRACTICALITY – Practicality is a mantra by which a Concrete Sequential person lives their life. If it is impractical, it teeters on the edge of being useless.

PREDICTABILITY – Whereas routines are the lifeblood of this type of thinker, predictability is the oxygen that fuels the blood. Knowing that 1+1 will always equal 2 is not a nice-to-know; it is a universal truth.

 **CHALLENGES:**

GROUPS – Concrete Sequential thinkers tend to be lone wolves. They are typically frustrated by the interplay of groups and group dynamics. These thinkers would much rather be on their own, where control is entirely within their grasp.

DISORGANIZATION – Probably the most frustrating and irritating aspect of what is brought into their world from the outside and outsiders. This disorganized intrusion will irritate even the best of this type of thinker.

AMBIGUITY – These instances violate the natural order of their world and their life. When 1+1 does not necessarily equal 2 due to some unusual situation or circumstance, their world is shaken to its core.

ABSTRACTNESS – In this thinker's world, there is no such event as an abstract event. Abstractness is typically not allowed within the confines of their daily life or world, not in any way, shape, or form—EVER.

A visual summary of the Concrete Sequential Mind/Thinking Style may be found in Figure 2.5.

CONCRETE SEQUENTIAL - LIKES, IDEALS & CHALLENGES

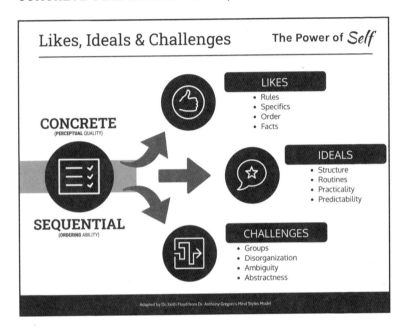

Figure 2.5

With the insights gained regarding the Concrete Sequential Mind/Thinking Style, take a moment to complete Reflection 2.2. In addition, if the Concrete Sequential style is aligned with your respective perceptual quality and ordering ability, complete the additional self-reflection activity found in Reflection 2.3.

 **REFLECTION**

1. What's resonating with or landing on you regarding this thinking style type?

_____

_____

_____

_____

_____

2. Were there any surprises? If so, what were they?

_____

_____

_____

_____

_____

3. What will you now do with the insights and knowledge gained through this exploration?

_____

_____

_____

_____

_____

Reflection 2.2

If the Concrete Sequential Mind/Thinking Style is aligned with your style of thinking and learning, please reflect upon and answer the following additional questions:

SELF-REFLECTION

1. Where and when has this type of thinking benefited you the most? Explain.

_____

_____

_____

_____

_____

2. Where and when has this type of thinking hindered you the most? Explain.

_____

_____

_____

_____

_____

3. If you were given the opportunity to explain to someone how you see, process, think about, and learn best within this world—to better help them understand you and how you "tick"—in just one sentence, what would that sentence be?

_____

_____

_____

_____

_____

Reflection 2.3 (CONCRETE SEQUENTIAL Thinkers – **ONLY**)

Concrete
Random

MIND/THINKING STYLE:
CONCRETE RANDOM

This individual, while still being based in reality, also has the capability for visionary thinking and is willing to experiment with ideas to allow their vision to come to fruition.

THIS THINKER:

 **LIKES:**

VISION – Vision is a centerpiece for this type of thinker. Developing and knowing the "Big Picture" and being able to communicate this picture is of utmost importance to them.

EXPERIMENTING – This type of thinker revels in trial and error and uses this space as a stepping stone to discovery. Even though their perceptual quality is concrete, the opportunity to speculate and ask "What if?" energizes them.

CREATIVITY – Creativity and the creative process are the fuel that sustains the fire that burns within this thinker (learner). The ability to create something new that did not exist before is exhilarating.

PROBLEM-SOLVING – A Concrete Random thinker is not afraid of problems. On the contrary, they are intrigued by problems and are driven by the challenge of solving them.

IDEALS:

EXPLORING – Much like the drive within the world's great explorers, this thinker (learner) thrives on adventure and searching for lost or new things. In addition, they are continually on a quest for themes to make new and deeper connections.

TAKING RISKS – Whereas most people are risk-averse, this style type has no issues with stepping into the unknown and taking a chance.

POSSIBILITIES – This thinker (learner) loves options and possibilities. In addition, they see possibilities everywhere—due to their creative mindset and their affinity toward exploration.

INNOVATION – The chance to create something new or different by connecting disparate ideas or things drives this thinker/learner. These thinkers are the ones who typically "change the world" with their new ideas and products.

CHALLENGES:

LIMITS – With a creative and innovative mindset, this thinker is annoyed by limits (either real or perceived), for they interrupt the flow of their creative process.

RESTRICTIONS – Although similar in nature to limits, restrictions are even worse, for they actually *prevent* this mind type from possibilities they have yet to discover.

DETAILS – Whereas being a "Big Picture" person and thinker is strongly within their wheelhouse, details are their "Kryptonite." This thinker/learner typically needs support with specifics and assistance with follow-through.

ROUTINES – Unlike their Concrete Sequential counterparts (individuals who love routines), a Concrete Random individual feels constrained by routines and instead gravitates toward spontaneous and free-spirited endeavors.

A visual summary of the Concrete Random Mind/Thinking Style may be found in Figure 2.6.

CONCRETE RANDOM - LIKES, IDEALS & CHALLENGES

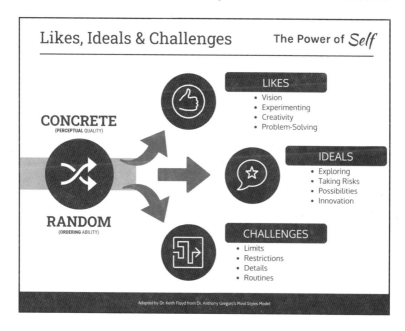

Figure 2.6

With the insights gained regarding the Concrete Random Mind/Thinking Style, take a moment to complete Reflection 2.4. In addition, if the Concrete Random style aligns with your respective perceptual quality and ordering ability, complete the additional self-reflection activity found in Reflection 2.5.

 **REFLECTION**

1. What's resonating with or landing on you regarding this
   thinking style type?

   _____

   _____

   _____

   _____

   _____

2. Were there any surprises? If so, what were they?

   _____

   _____

   _____

   _____

   _____

3. What will you now do with the insights and knowledge
   gained through this exploration?

   _____

   _____

   _____

   _____

   _____

Reflection 2.4

If the Concrete Random Mind/Thinking Style is aligned
with your style of thinking and learning, please reflect upon
and answer the following additional questions:

 SELF-REFLECTION

1. Where and when has this type of thinking benefited you the most? Explain.

_____

_____

_____

_____

_____

2. Where and when has this type of thinking hindered you the most? Explain.

_____

_____

_____

_____

_____

3. If you were given the opportunity to explain to someone how you see, process, think about, and learn best within this world—to better help them understand you and how you "tick"—in just one sentence, what would that sentence be?

_____

_____

_____

_____

_____

Reflection 2.5 (CONCRETE RANDOM Thinkers – **ONLY**)

Abstract
Random

MIND/THINKING STYLE:
ABSTRACT RANDOM

This individual thrives in unstructured and undefined (people-oriented) environments where non-linear thinking is the norm.

THIS THINKER:

 **LIKES:**

LISTENING – This thinker/learner is strongly aligned with the 80/20 Rule: listening 80% of the time and speaking 20% of the time. In doing so, they fully connect with others and are viewed as caring, supportive, and helpful.

BEING ENGAGED – Due in part to their ability to listen intently (and with purpose), this thinker/learner can focus on the present moment, stay fully engaged with others, and make deeper connections in the process.

RELATIONSHIPS – Their ability to listen intently and be fully engaged with others (and in situations) allows this thinker/learner to make and develop strong, long-lasting relationships.

PROCESS – This style of thinker enjoys "The Process" of things. Specifically, they enjoy being in and building upon the ideas of others in non-competitive, approachable ways.

 **IDEALS:**

FREEDOM – As an outgrowth of their ability to build strong relation-ships with others (in a non-competitive way), this thinker/learner can move within and around ideas, constructs, and groups.

FLEXIBILITY – A close cousin to "Freedom," flexibility for this thinker/learner is a cornerstone of their being. This is due in large part to the intersection and synergy of how they perceive and order their world in a *random* and *abstract* fashion.

GROUPS – Abstract Random individuals LOVE groups! They flourish and grow in group environments. Their natural ability to make connec-tions and develop relationships perfectly suits group settings.

HARMONY – Abstract Random individuals are natural peacekeepers. Their "likable" nature and ability to quickly gain the trust of others, through their heightened listening skills and capacity to "see all sides," allows them (and others) to function more comfortably and harmoniously.

 **CHALLENGES:**

RESTRICTIONS – Much like their Concrete Random cousins, Abstract Random individuals are troubled by restrictions. The difference is that they are only "troubled" by restrictions, whereas their cousins see restrictions as prohibitive.

COMPETITION – By nature, Abstract Random thinkers and learners are extremely *non-competitive*, so when situations arise requiring them to be competitive, their world is "turned on its head," and they must navigate in unfamiliar waters.

DISCORD – Discord is like *fingernails on a chalkboard* (an annoying, unpleasant, and uncomfortable sound) for this style type.[26] This "cringe-worthy" sensation is the contextual equivalent to Discord for Abstract Random thinkers and learners.

SAYING "NO" – With the desire to connect, relate, and support others, this style type may have difficulty "saying no" to the requests and demands of those within their network. In addition, if left unchecked, this thinker/learner type may knowingly or unknowingly be taken advantage of by their more needy and demanding network connection.

A visual summary of the Abstract Random Mind/Thinking Style may be found in Figure 2.7.

ABSTRACT RANDOM - LIKES, IDEALS & CHALLENGES

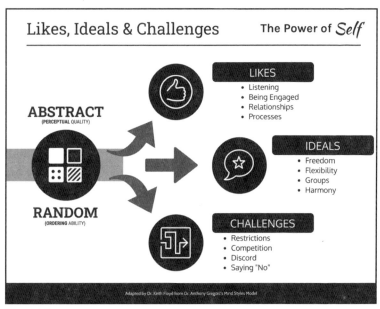

Figure 2.7

With the insights gained regarding the Abstract Random Mind/Thinking Style, take a moment to complete Reflection 2.6. In addition, if the Abstract Random style is aligned with your respective perceptual quality and ordering ability, complete the additional self-reflection activity found in Reflection 2.7.

 **REFLECTION**

1. What's resonating with or landing on you regarding this
   thinking style type?

   _____

   _____

   _____

   _____

   _____

2. Were there any surprises? If so, what were they?

   _____

   _____

   _____

   _____

   _____

3. What will you now do with the insights and knowledge
   gained through this exploration?

   _____

   _____

   _____

   _____

   _____

Reflection 2.6

If the Abstract Random Mind/Thinking Style is aligned
with your style of thinking and learning, please reflect upon
and answer the following additional questions:

 SELF-REFLECTION

1. Where and when has this type of thinking benefited you the
   most? Explain.

   _____

   _____

   _____

   _____

   _____

2. Where and when has this type of thinking hindered you the
   most? Explain.

   _____

   _____

   _____

   _____

   _____

3. If you were given the opportunity to explain to someone how
   you see, process, think about, and learn best within this
   world—to better help them understand you and how you
   "tick"—in just one sentence, what would that sentence be?

   _____

   _____

   _____

   _____

   _____

Reflection 2.7 (ABSTRACT RANDOM Thinkers – **ONLY**)

MIND/THINKING STYLE:
ABSTRACT SEQUENTIAL

Abstract
Sequential

While still embracing many of the benefits of flexible environments, this individual also gravitates toward theory, data, and analysis.

THIS THINKER:

 **LIKES:**

DATA – To the Abstract Sequential thinker, data is the foundation of everything. They are strongly rooted in facts and figures and utilize data as their proverbial "compass" to guide them along and through their respective journeys.

ANALYSIS – This thinker is careful and deliberate in all they do, basing their decisions on their analysis of the data they have collected or have been given.

LOGIC – Combining their aptitude and affinity for data and analysis, their use of logic is a natural outgrowth and outcome of the melding of their need for data and analysis. In doing so, they tend to curtail their expressions of emotions and prefer a more logic-based world.

BEING HEARD – Knowing that they have detailed facts and figures "on their side," these thinkers wish to be heard to prove their point, and will be persistent until they have an opportunity to share their insights and make their point known.

 **IDEALS:**

CHALLENGES – Challenges are a great way to engage with this thinking type, especially when the challenge involves data, traditions, and historical perspectives aligned with proven procedures and guidelines that are very deliberate in nature.

RESEARCH – A key part of research is "asking the question" and then carefully weighing all sides of a problem or issue in a balanced and logical manner, utilizing the best of themselves and their skills to come to a careful and objective conclusion.

PLAYING "DEVIL'S ADVOCATE" – This thinker (largely based upon their experiences and attention to details, steps, and procedures) can play the "Devil's Advocate" exquisitely. This thinker is incredibly skilled at finding the so-called "fatal flaw" in the thinking, plans, or procedures of others.

FINDING SOLUTIONS – Due to their natural ability to be organized and objective (again based largely on their fondness for data and analysis), they can find solutions that are not typically apparent at first glance.

 **CHALLENGES:**

TRIVIAL TASKS – Solidly grounded in a world of facts and figures—where processes and procedures are done so on purpose, and with a specific intent - this thinking style finds any task that falls into the realm of the trivial or frivolous to be completely unbearable and an absolute waste of time.

BEING OVER-REGULATED – The only structure this thinking type needs is housed in their data and analysis. Anything beyond this is viewed as an over-regulation and an outright intrusion into their work and universe.

TIME CONSTRAINTS – One of the key tenets for this thinker (learner) is time. This thinker and learner type needs time to research, calculate, and process the information they have either at hand or are searching out. Pressing this individual to conform to a timeframe and timeline other than their own creation is too oppressive.

EXPRESSING EMOTIONS – Much like the fictional Star Fleet Science Officer, Mr. Spock, this thinker/learner is sometimes challenged with emotions and their various expressions. Again, being anchored in facts, figures, and large-scale data, this individual is composed and fascinated by logic.

A visual summary of the Abstract Sequential Mind/ Thinking Style may be found in Figure 2.8.

ABSTRACT SEQUENTIAL - LIKES, IDEALS & CHALLENGES

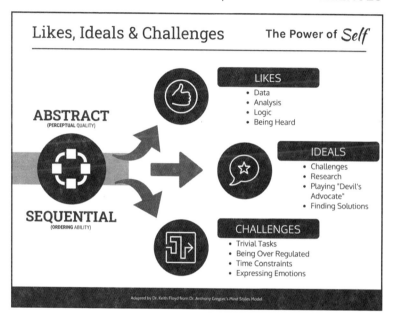

Figure 2.8

With the insights gained regarding the Abstract Sequential Mind/Thinking Style, take a moment to complete Reflection 2.8. In addition, if the Abstract Sequential style is aligned with your respective perceptual quality and ordering ability, complete the additional self-reflection activity in Reflection 2.9.

 **REFLECTION**

1. What's resonating with or landing on you regarding this
   thinking style type?

_____

_____

_____

_____

_____

2. Were there any surprises? If so, what were they?

_____

_____

_____

_____

_____

3. What will you now do with the insights and knowledge
   gained through this exploration?

_____

_____

_____

_____

_____

Reflection 2.8

If the Abstract Sequential Mind/Thinking Style is aligned
with your style of thinking and learning, please reflect upon
and answer the following additional questions:

 SELF-REFLECTION

1. Where and when has this type of thinking benefited you the most? Explain.

_____

_____

_____

_____

_____

2. Where and when has this type of thinking hindered you the most? Explain.

_____

_____

_____

_____

_____

3. If you were given the opportunity to explain to someone how you see, process, think about, and learn best within this world—to better help them understand you and how you "tick"—in just one sentence, what would that sentence be?

_____

_____

_____

_____

_____

Reflection 2.9 (ABSTRACT SEQUENTIAL Thinkers – **ONLY**)

The information and construct of the mind/thinking styles are a lot to take in at once. Still, it is an excellent tool and resource to assist in determining and explaining how and why you think, process, and act within this world. The Likes, Ideals, and Challenges are profoundly insightful and allow for a sense of understanding—possibly for the first time—and are incredibly valuable. A possession that will benefit you and others in countless ways. The ability to identify and then process each of these styles is exactly what will be explored next as you analyze and examine how this knowledge about yourself and others helps guide you throughout your life.

HOW IT GUIDES YOU

In 1921, Swiss psychologist Hermann Rorschach developed a test where he would show an individual an indiscriminate image, a blot of ink on a piece of paper, and then ask the individual to describe what they saw. This test, which is called The Rorschach Inkblot Test, per its creator and design, rose in popularity across the psychological community in the decades that followed, reaching its peak popularity during the 1960s, and has been utilized countless times to gain insight into a person's perceptions and psychological state.[27] In essence, it helps the assessor and the individual being assessed to gain understanding and context regarding what the individual is seeing and thinking.

This one-hundred-year-old assessment is a lens through which to view and be viewed. Using this context of a lens, the late Alan Peshkin (former Professor of Education at Stanford University) penned a research article in the *Journal of Qualitative Inquiry*, which was published soon after his death in 2000. In his article, Peshkin asserts that "lenses provide a means of opening into or looking into" and that "each lens holds the promise of seeing what is useful." When we gain newfound insights into how we and others perceive, think, and process the world, we can use that knowledge to make better decisions, as Peshkin suggests:

> *...prepare the mind to overcome the sensory shutdown that results from being in the same place for a long time, like running on a treadmill. If we fall victim to the limitations of our perceptual locations, it is time to move on and adopt another lens.*

Peshkin says that we tend to get into a "routine," and once in that routine, we tend to see things only from that perspective—like having the same view while "running on a treadmill." Too often, we tend to get "stuck" in a singular line of thinking about issues and the world around us.[28] But this does not have to be the case, and this does not have to be a permanent event.

We have the ability, if we allow ourselves, to gain new lenses to be able to see ourselves and those around us in new and different ways. In ways that allow us (allow you) to better understand how *you* think about and process the world, and going one step further, taking these same lenses to gain understanding of the perspectives of others. But how do you see the world through someone else's lens and from their perspective? The short answer is that you need to be educated on how best to prepare your mind to see yourself and others differently.

Richard T. Barber, a professor emeritus of biological oceanography from Duke University, and a contemporary of Peshkin, in the context of lenses and their duty and effectiveness stated, "If your mind is not prepared, it doesn't matter what you look at. You don't see it." More often than not, people tend to see the world through only one lens, and more importantly, they tend to think that everyone else sees the world the same way they do. But this is not the case, not even by a long shot. We are all different; we see the world differently, and make decisions daily based on what we know and how we see the world around us. The fact that we must be prepared (in mind) to see what is there, even if it is not immediately visible, is paramount. This acknowledgment will be the stepping-off point for how your newly "prepared mind" will allow you to see things you may not have seen before, and more importantly, understand how it guides you (and others) daily.

In the following paragraphs and pages, you will be given two scenarios that are very similar in nature yet also very different. In the first scenario, you will be presented with a problem that is unfortunately all too real for too many people and is a problem that you may encounter within your everyday personal life. You will be required to think about and then develop a plan of action as to how you will solve this problem utilizing the insights gained by means of your respective lens and thinking style. In addition, and utilizing the remaining three mind/thinking styles, you will then be asked to speculate how other thinking styles would go about generating a solution to this same problem, but from their respective lens.

SCENARIO 1
PERSONAL LIFE

You live in the Northeast; it's wintertime and very cold outside. You wake up early in the morning to see your breath in the air. You go to the thermostat, and it reads 45 degrees. You check your furnace and discover that it's not running or working. You own your own home, so there is no landlord or building superintendent you can call. In addition, and to make matters worse, your car is in the shop and potentially needs four new tires to pass inspection. You're also running low on groceries, so you need to go to the store for food. You have two small mouths to feed, and you only have $472.53 in your checking account with another 10 days until your next payday. Utilizing Figure 2.9, the downloaded form from *The Power of Self* website (www.ThePowerofSelfbook.com) or the space provided, answer the following questions:

1. How will you solve this series of compounding problems from your mind/thinking style? Outline your plan of action and provide a brief explanation for each decision (i.e., why you chose this course of action as opposed to another).

_____
_____
_____
_____
_____
_____
_____
_____

2. After finishing your plan and explanations, imagine yourself in the same situation, but this time, try to view the problem through the lenses of the remaining three mind/thinking styles. Speculate on how your peers with different thinking styles would approach and solve the same problems from their point of view and using their unique perspectives.

STYLE 1:_____

_____

_____

_____

_____

_____

_____

STYLE 2:_____

_____

_____

_____

_____

_____

_____

STYLE 3:_____

_____

_____

_____

_____

_____

_____

SCENARIO 1 - PERSONAL LIFE WORKSHEET

SCENARIO 1 - PERSONAL LIFE The Power of *Self*			
Concrete Sequential	Concrete Random	Abstract Random	Abstract Sequential
HOW?	HOW?	HOW?	HOW?
WHY?	WHY?	WHY?	WHY?

Figure 2.9

Utilizing the insights gained through this activity, complete Reflection 2.10.

REFLECTION

1. What did you learn about yourself, and how does your mind/ thinking style guide you?

_____

_____

_____

_____

_____

2. How challenging was it to place yourself into another mind/ thinking style—seeing the same event but through that respective lens while attempting to problem-solve from that perspective? Explain.

_____

_____

_____

_____

_____

3. How will you use the insights gained about yourself, your mind/ thinking style, as well as others and their styles going forward?

_____

_____

_____

_____

_____

Reflection 2.10

Utilizing the approach you used to complete the Personal Life scenario, follow the same processes, but now from a work perspective.

SCENARIO 2
WORK LIFE

You work in a medium- to large-sized company, and the company has had some financial challenges in recent months—work stoppages, material and supply shortages, as well as personnel and cashflow shortages. Additionally, you still have five months to go in your budgetary year until the next new large projects are scheduled to begin. You have been tasked by your supervisor to reduce your total budget and expenses by 20% for the remaining months of the budgetary year. You must present your recommendations on this complex issue to the executive leadership of the company within the next three days. Utilizing Figure 2.10, the downloaded form from *The Power of Self* website (www.ThePowerofSelfbook.com), or the space provided, answer the following questions:

1. How will you solve this series of compounding problems from your mind/thinking style? Outline your plan of action and provide a brief explanation for each decision (i.e., why you chose this course of action as opposed to another).

_____

_____

_____

_____

_____

_____

_____

_____

2. After finishing your plan and explanations, imagine yourself in the same situation, but this time, try to view the problem through the lenses of the remaining three mind/thinking styles. Speculate on how your peers with different thinking styles would approach and solve the same problems from their point of view and using their unique perspectives.

STYLE 1: _____

_____

_____

_____

_____

_____

_____

_____

STYLE 2: _____

_____

_____

_____

_____

_____

_____

_____

STYLE 3: _____

_____

_____

_____

_____

_____

_____

_____

SCENARIO 2 - WORK LIFE WORKSHEET

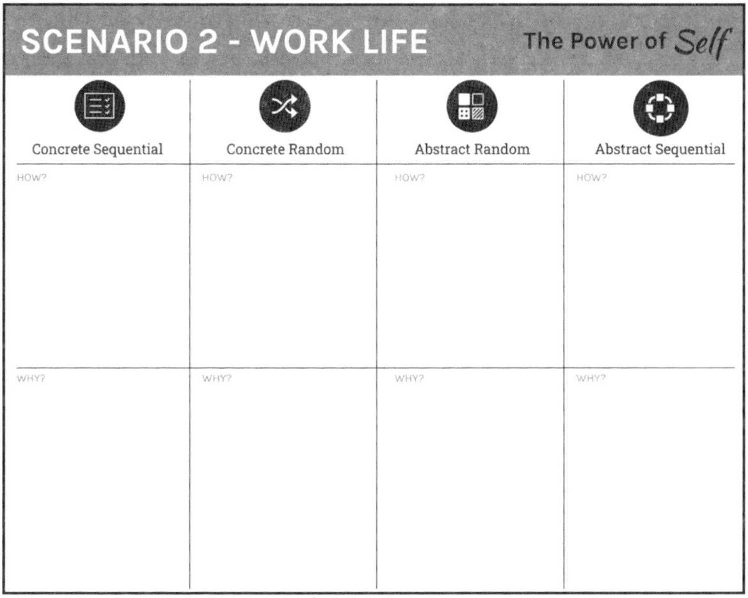

SCENARIO 2 - WORK LIFE			The Power of *Self*
Concrete Sequential	Concrete Random	Abstract Random	Abstract Sequential
HOW?	HOW?	HOW?	HOW?
WHY?	WHY?	WHY?	WHY?

Figure 2.10

Utilizing the insights gained through this activity, complete Reflection 2.11.

REFLECTION

1. What did you learn about yourself, and how does your mind/ thinking style guide you?

_____

_____

_____

_____

_____

2. How challenging was it to place yourself into another mind/
   thinking style—seeing the same event but through that
   respective lens while attempting to problem-solve from that
   perspective? Explain.

_____

_____

_____

_____

_____

3. How will you use the insights gained about yourself, your mind/
   thinking style, as well as others and their styles going forward?

_____

_____

_____

_____

_____

Reflection 2.11

The journey that you are on is an ever-evolving one.
During this journey, you are not only learning about yourself,
your thinking, and how it guides you, you are also learning
and gaining insights into how others see the world and are
guided by their thinking. This appreciation and understanding
of others and the lenses they use to view their world is a form
of empathic understanding.

Carl Rogers, renowned psychologist and humanist,
penned a research article in 1975 entitled "Empathic: An
Unappreciated Way of Being." In this article, Rogers states
that "empathy is correlated with self-exploration," just as you

are doing at this present moment. He goes on to state that "empathy early in the relationship predicts later success," much like you being able to connect with your respective mind/thinking style and understanding how it guides you, as well as connecting with others and more fully understanding their perspective and the way their style guides them. This understanding and engagement are crucial and, with practice, can be more fully developed. Rogers stated that "perhaps the most important statement of all is that the ability to be accurately empathic is something which can be developed by training." Training that will allow you to see, think, and understand yourself and others more fully and accurately.[29]

When you couple the views and thinking of others with your own discoveries, your view of the world becomes very different. The activities and the collective learnings you are making in these very moments are key to you becoming the true *authentic* you, preparing you and your mind for the next iterations of you. Louis Pasteur, renowned French chemist, famously said, "Where observation is concerned, chance favors only the prepared mind." Through these recent exercises, you are "preparing your mind" for not only you, but for the betterment of others, through your observations, understandings, and ability to consider how they see and think about the world. By challenging yourself to consider various perspectives, you can greatly enhance your own way of thinking and broaden your understanding. This practice of opening your mind to different lenses is key to unlocking your full potential and living your best life.

What you think, how you think it, and how you make

sense of this thinking is the core of your self-concept. A self-concept that requires time, insight, and attention to fully come into being. A *you* that is based upon who you truly are, and not what others think or perceive you to be. A *you* that is constantly learning and evolving but doing so based upon what you know about yourself and not fulfilling some other person's prophecy of you. As you will soon see, this evolution (and the evolutions to come) is built upon a foundation of the causes that you hold most dear, the beliefs that ground and guide you, and the purpose that you are placed on this planet to pursue. A foundation currently housed deep inside the confines of *you*. A *you* that is rooted and guided by the things you stand for—your causes, your beliefs, and your why. A triad of such profound magnitude and importance, each allowing for an even deeper awareness and understanding of who you truly are, as well as the bonus of a deeper awareness and understanding of those around you, and in the process, creating a level of self-understanding which is ushering you yet another step closer to your *true authentic self.*

PART 2: SELF-CONCEPT
IN SUMMARY

If someone thinks that you will act and behave in a certain way when you're together, they will make you act and behave exactly that way through their interactions with you. They will also make you act and behave the same way when you are with other people. Sound ridiculous or impossible? It's not ridiculous or impossible—it's true. Without a firm grasp of your own self-concept, you will leave yourself open to being either consciously or unconsciously manipulated by all the people with whom you interact. This is a hard truth to accept, but it is true nonetheless, unless you know who you truly are and have a firm grasp of your own self-concept. In this context, self–concept involves knowing how you think, why you think it, and how this way of thinking guides you.

Knowing how you think and being able to name and understand this way of thinking is the first step to a stronger self-concept. Are you a Concrete Sequential thinker? Or a Concrete Random thinker? An Abstract Random or an Abstract Sequential thinker? And what is meant by each of the four thinking styles? A Concreate Sequential thinker is someone who is based in reality and sees the world very logically. A Concrete Random person is some-one who also likes reality, but likes to experiment and bring new visions to life. An Abstract Random thinker is someone who likes people and likes the freedom to do things differently. And the Abstract Sequential person is someone who likes flexibility, but still keeps facts and data in hand to prove their points. Once you know how you think, you also need to understand why you think this way.

Why you think a certain way is a little more involved and takes a little more time to process. Why you think the way you do involves understanding the things that you "like" about thinking this way, things that are "ideal" for you and help you be successful, but also acknowledge and address the aspects that "challenge" you as a thinker and how you engage with others and the world. Understanding why you think a certain way is a stepping-stone to understanding how it also guides you in this world.

How your thinking guides you is the culmination of how and why you think that way in the first place. This culmination will lead you to look at and process your world differently. Opening yourself up to not only gaining insight into how it guides you, but also gaining insight into how other thinking styles are guided by how they see and think about their worlds. Seeing the world through another person's eyes—through their lens—allows you to empathize and connect with that person and, in turn, gives you even greater insight into yourself. This greater insight or awareness allows you to travel even further on your journey of discovery by moving you even closer to your true *authentic self.*

SO NOW WHAT?
(ACTION STEPS)

ACTION STEP 1: **HOW YOU THINK**

Use your newfound knowledge about how you see and think about your world and the world around you as an opportunity —a starting point—rather than a destination.

ACTION STEP 2: **WHY YOU THINK IT**

Knowing your likes, ideals, and challenges allows you to navigate your world more effectively, so lean into your likes, cultivate your ideals, and accept your challenges for what they are.

ACTION STEP 3: **HOW IT GUIDES YOU**

Use the awareness of how your thinking style guides you to move you closer to your true authentic self, but also use what you've learned to better connect and engage with others.

SELF: PART 3

KNOW WHAT YOU STAND FOR:
THE POWER OF SELF-UNDERSTANDING

*"Authenticity is when you say and do
the things you actually believe."*
- Simon Sinek

In Act I, Scene III of *Hamlet*, considered one of William Shakespeare's greatest works, Shakespeare provides us with one of the greatest lines in English literature regarding being your true self and allowing this knowledge to guide you. In the scene, Polonius, the father of Laertes, says to his son as he prepares to board a boat and travel to Paris, *"This above all: to thine own self be true, and it must follow, as the night the day, thou canst not then be false to any man."* [30] At this moment, Polonius is counseling his son to "stay true to himself" and to what guides him—his principles and purpose—instead of being influenced and "led astray" by others. This being "led astray," as we now know by way of Fazio, Effrein, and Falender's study, can happen very easily. This piece of personal advice and the wisdom that comes with it is just one piece of the puzzle that leads to self-understanding.

In 1998, the now-late Yale University professor and Shakespearean expert Harold Bloom wrote a book entitled *Shakespeare: The Invention of the Human.* In his book, Bloom shares a relative chronology of William Shakespeare and his works, encompassing his early works through his most seminal later works, specifically exploring and unraveling the various aspects of humanity as each pertains to the evolution and development of people. This development of people is conducted through the lens of Shakespeare's multifaceted characters. Characters through Shakespeare's collected works demonstrated the near full breadth of human behaviors and experiences, along with profoundly keen insights into the inner workings of man. Shakespeare had the gift and ability to present new and unique insights into humanity through his words and characters. Insights that had never been named in literature until that moment were the foundation of what would later become much of Sigmund Freud's, and his con-temporaries', theories and work. In Bloom's prologue to his book, he demonstrates how the collective of Shakespearean characters act as newfound guides to the rest of humanity, showing us how humanity can be more "human" by growing and evolving into the next best versions of ourselves through discovery, development, and most importantly—through self-understanding. Quoting Bloom:

> *In Shakespeare, characters develop rather than unfold, and they develop because they reconceive themselves. Sometimes this comes about because they overhear themselves talking, whether to themselves or to others. Self-overhearing is their royal road to individuation, and no other writer, before or since Shakespeare, has accomplished so well the virtual miracle of creating utterly different yet self-consistent voices for his more than one hundred major characters and many hundreds of highly distinctive minor personages.*[31]

What Bloom is saying is that Shakespeare's characters are not just what they appear to be on the surface, but they actually "develop" and become something new and, at times, unexpected—just as each of us does throughout the course of our individual life stories. And in the process of doing so, Shakespeare's characters, as well as every one of us, in turn, gain the knowledge and understanding of who we are and the world around us. Through this discovery process, we are able, as Bloom states, to "reconceive" ourselves, just as you are currently doing in the context of your journey to authenticity through the explorations and exercises within this book. This understanding, this *true understanding* of who you are, is conceived and gained by tapping into the power of self-understanding by uncovering and discovering the aspects of your life that become the "causes" that you hold most dear, by the "beliefs" that guide you, and lastly by the purpose or "why" that drives you. The intersection of these three key tenets that reside deep inside of you and may have yet to be fully discovered are three of the most powerful guiding forces that you will ever know in your lifetime. Forces that will allow you to live *with confidence* the charge put forth by Shakespeare and through the words of his muse Polonius when he reminded Laertes, "To thine own self be true." This is a truth that you will hopefully now discover, or possibly even rediscover, in the following exercises, through your purposeful work, and through the deep reflections you will engage in.

YOUR CAUSES

Simon Sinek, the author of the quote at the onset of this section, is also the author of a profoundly insightful book entitled *Start With Why: How Great Leaders Inspire Everyone To Take Action*. In his book, Sinek describes what he has coined as "The Golden Circle." The Golden Circle, in actuality, is comprised of three circles, each inside the next, which is, in essence, a bullseye.[32] Take a moment and construct a mental image of a bullseye comprised of three circles interlaid upon one another in your mind. With this image now established, I will label each of the respective rings utilizing Sinek. The outer ring of the bullseye is classified or labeled with the word "What." Moving inward, the next ring, or the middle ring, is classified or labeled with the word "How." And the final, innermost ring, the bullseye itself, is labeled as "Why." I will briefly explain the meanings for each of the circles momentarily, but in the interim, I strongly suggest that you watch Sinek's TEDxPuget Sound from September 2009. His TEDx session is only 18 minutes long, during which he provides deeper context to The Golden Circles and the implications of their use. You may access the session through the following link: https://www.ted.com/talks/simon_sinek_how_great_leaders_inspire_action?language=en, or you may simply Google "Simon Sinek Golden Circle" with the first video listed being his 2009 session.[33]

In his TEDx talk, Sinek, using his Golden Circle image, summarizes his book's principles and content. Sinek uses examples ranging from the Apple Corporation to the Wright brothers, and even the Reverend Dr. Martin Luther King Jr. to explain that almost any person or company on this planet can tell you "What they do." Most can also tell you "How they do it." But only a very few of these individuals, companies, or groups can tell you "Why they do it." But why is that?

As he explains, the reason for this extremely small group of individuals and groups with a keen understanding and articulation of "their why," is largely due to the function of the human brain and our respective biology. Here's why and how. Deep within your brain is a structure called the limbic system. This system is responsible for your feelings, motivations, and emotions—the mainstays of your personal drive. But here is the rub: This same system that helps to guide you and your feelings and emotions has an extremely limited capacity for language. For example, if someone asks you for your opinion on something you feel strongly about. You may typically say something like, "I can't really explain it. It's just a feeling." The challenge in finding the words to describe your feeling is due to your entrance into your limbic system and the connection to the context of feelings you are attempting to articulate. This system—this part of you—is where many of the "whys" in your life and the world reside. This place—the literal bullseye of Sinek's Golden Circle—is where your feelings and emotions reside for the "causes" you hold most dear.

With this newfound knowledge, image, and context, we will explore the causes you hold most dear. To accomplish this, you will work through your next reflection exercise. This reflection will require you to dig a little deeper into who you are and will also require you to write down what you stand for—*your causes*. A task or reflection that you may have never given purposeful time to reflect upon, let alone attempting to write these reflections down. In essence, declaring what your causes happen to be. Based upon the information gained from Simon Sinek's Golden Circle and striving to drill down and find this portion of your "why" by means of the "causes" you hold most dear, please reflect upon and answer the following questions, in exact order, to aid you in being able to articulate the causes that drive you. Utilizing Reflection 3.1 and Figure 3.1, please answer the following questions:

 **REFLECTION**

1. What are the things that motivate you to act?

_____

_____

_____

_____

_____

2. What are the principles and ideals that drive you forward?

_____

_____

_____

_____

_____

3. Reflecting on and interpreting the answers from your responses to Questions 1 and 2, what are the specific causes that you hold most dear?

   (Note: After answering this question, transfer your responses to Question 1 onto the Why Statement Frayer Diagram in Figure 3.1 or onto the other document option choice referenced earlier)

_____

_____

_____

_____

_____

Reflection 3.1

Causes are deeply rooted and deeply personal aspects of who you are. They are the things that allow your emotions and passions to come to the surface. They are the things that often allow your altruistic, selfless nature to be seen and become self-evident. They are the things that help to drive you and your beliefs and convictions. They align with the principles and ideals that go beyond the boundaries of everyday work and life. This acknowledgement, understanding, and now declaration, and using your written responses to the question "What are the specific causes that you hold most dear?" are the forces that will allow a more authentic you to be seen—much like Mr. Rogers and his cause to see children learn and grow in a caring and loving environment. This environment recognized them as gifts, and with the enduring hope that this foundation would allow them to grow and become understanding, loving, and productive members of society.

These are causes worth pursuing. But causes are only one piece of the *why puzzle*. The next piece to the puzzle consists of the beliefs guiding you along your daily journeys and life. Beliefs that, when coupled with your causes, can become powerful portions of who you are and take you another step closer to gaining a *true understanding* of yourself and another step closer to your *true authentic self*. A step that includes exploring and declaring your beliefs and how these beliefs guide you.

YOUR BELIEFS

On December 10, 1964, the Reverend Dr. Martin Luther

King Jr., during his Nobel Peace Prize acceptance speech in
Oslo, Norway, shared one of the most powerful belief statements ever put forth when he proclaimed to all those in atten-
dance and the world, his belief about the powers of good
versus evil, right versus wrong, and love versus hate when
he stated, *"I believe that unarmed truth and unconditional
love will have the final word in reality. That is why right,
temporarily defeated, is stronger than evil triumphant."* [34]
These 26 words put forth by Dr. King demonstrated his belief
that no matter what may occur, even temporary defeats at the
hands of evil, evil may not overtake the freedom of the truth
and the power and strength of "unconditional love."

Through his beliefs and his life's work, Dr. King continuously strived to put forward his desire for a better life and a
better world for all. But to do so, he first and foremost needed
to know what those beliefs were and understand how strongly
they guided him. Beliefs that were developed and tested
through his own life and experiences, as well as those who
were impacted by the grave injustices that befell African-
Americans in the centuries leading up to and through the
American civil rights movement. Beliefs that continue to be
passed down, carrying on his legacy by those who share his
beliefs for generations to come.

Dr. King's legacy began with strong, deeply rooted
beliefs that are basic to human life, such as, citing Dr. King,
*"People everywhere can have three meals a day for their
bodies, education and culture for their minds, and dignity,
equality, and freedom for their spirits."* And on a larger scale
and for all humanity, his belief that *"we can transform dark*

yesterdays of injustice into bright tomorrows of justice and humanity." These are things worth believing in and causes worth fighting for.

This leads to the next, more direct question: *What do you believe?* Still keeping in mind Simon Sinek's bullseye *why*, the causes that you hold most dear, as well as the pretext of Dr. King and his strongly held beliefs, and utilizing Reflection 3.2, please reflect upon and answer the following questions to aid you in being able to articulate the beliefs that guide you.

 **REFLECTION**

1. What are the things in life that ground you?

_____

_____

_____

_____

_____

2. What are the things, or areas, within your life that you have firm opinions about or strong convictions for?

_____

_____

_____

_____

_____

3. Reflecting on and interpreting the answers from your responses to Questions 1 and 2, what are the specific causes that you hold most dear?

(Note: After answering this question, transfer your responses to Question 1 onto the Why Statement Frayer Diagram in Figure 3.1 or onto the other document option choice referenced earlier)

_____

_____

_____

_____

_____

Reflection 3.2

Beliefs are powerful pieces of who you are, what you strive to be, and what grounds and guides you throughout your life. Thinking about your beliefs in concert with your causes, truly reflect on each of these areas that make you, *you*. In addition, take a moment to reflect on how these aspects of you, when shared with and demonstrated to the world, allow for the true "authentic" you to be introduced. An introduction that is rooted in the core aspects of you and what you stand for. Even so, there is still one deeper, more personal piece of you to be discovered. The third and final piece—your purpose— your *why*. A *why* that drives you every day of your life. A *why* that motivates and explains your being on this planet, why you are destined to pursue your causes based upon your beliefs, and how these become the guiding force within your life. This *why* allows you to be your *true authentic self*, just like Mr. Rogers and Dr. Martin Luther King, Jr.

YOUR WHY

"To engage with and to cultivate people, so that they may become the persons that they are meant to be."

This brief, grammatically incorrect [persons should be people], yet purposeful, statement is my personal purpose or *why* statement. As stated, the error is purposeful. The persons you and I are today are not the people we were five or ten years ago. And the persons you and I will be in five or ten years from now are not the people we are today. We continuously grow and evolve into the next iteration, or version, of ourselves. As Bloom stated. and as Shakespeare allowed us to see, we "*develop rather than unfold…they [we] reconceive themselves [ourselves].*" This re-conception or discovery is the crux of your *why* statement. A statement that will allow you to articulate your why in just a few words. To accomplish this task, you will draw upon much of the work you have done in the earlier portions of this book and converge those insights with your more recent learnings.

Being authentic begins by "Being Honest" and "Being You," two enlightenments that hopefully have become clearer and more evident through the exercises, assessments, and reflections you have completed. These enlightenments and a keen understanding of your own personal *why* allow for the presentation of your *true authentic self.* Authenticity is nearly impossible to obtain without the knowledge and, more importantly, the understanding of these key facets. Luckily, you have already completed much of the heavy lifting to allow this clarity to come through due to your work in the previous portions of this book. To date, you have delineated your *causes*, acknowledged your *beliefs*, and have gained insights into your respective *contributions*. These three understandings will be the stepping stones to the final piece of information that will prepare you to craft your own personal *why statement*, the discovery of "How your contributions serve a greater purpose."

Considering all that you've learned about yourself and your respective "contributions," as well as the perspectives gained through your Contributions Partners, utilize Reflection 3.3 to answer the following questions:

 ## REFLECTION

1. List your personal and professional contributions using The 3-Words Method and the information gained by means of your self-reflection and the insights gifted to you by your Contributions Partners (Pages 37 and 38).

PERSONAL CONTRIBUTIONS

SELF:

1. _____
2. _____
3. _____

OTHERS:

1. _____   1. _____   1. _____
2. _____   2. _____   2. _____
3. _____   3. _____   3. _____

Name:_____   Name:_____   Name:_____

PROFESSIONAL CONTRIBUTIONS

SELF:

1. _____

2. _____

3. _____

OTHERS:

1. _____   1. _____   1. _____

2. _____   2. _____   2. _____

3. _____   3. _____   3. _____

Name:_____   Name:_____   Name:_____

2. Utilizing the responses from Reflection 3.3, Question 1, summarize your personal and professional contributions into one consolidated list of words and then answer the question: What are your (collective) contributions to this life?

   (Note: After answering this question, transfer your responses to Question 2 onto the Why Statement Frayer Diagram in Figure 3.1 or onto the other document option choices referenced earlier)

   _____
   _____
   _____
   _____
   _____

3. Reflecting on and interpreting the answers from your responses to Questions 1 and 2: How do these contributions serve a greater purpose?

   (Note: After answering this question, transfer your responses to Question 3 onto the Why Statement Frayer Diagram in Figure 3.1 or onto the other document option choices referenced earlier)

   _____
   _____
   _____
   _____
   _____

Reflection 3.3

FRAYER DIAGRAM: WHY STATEMENT

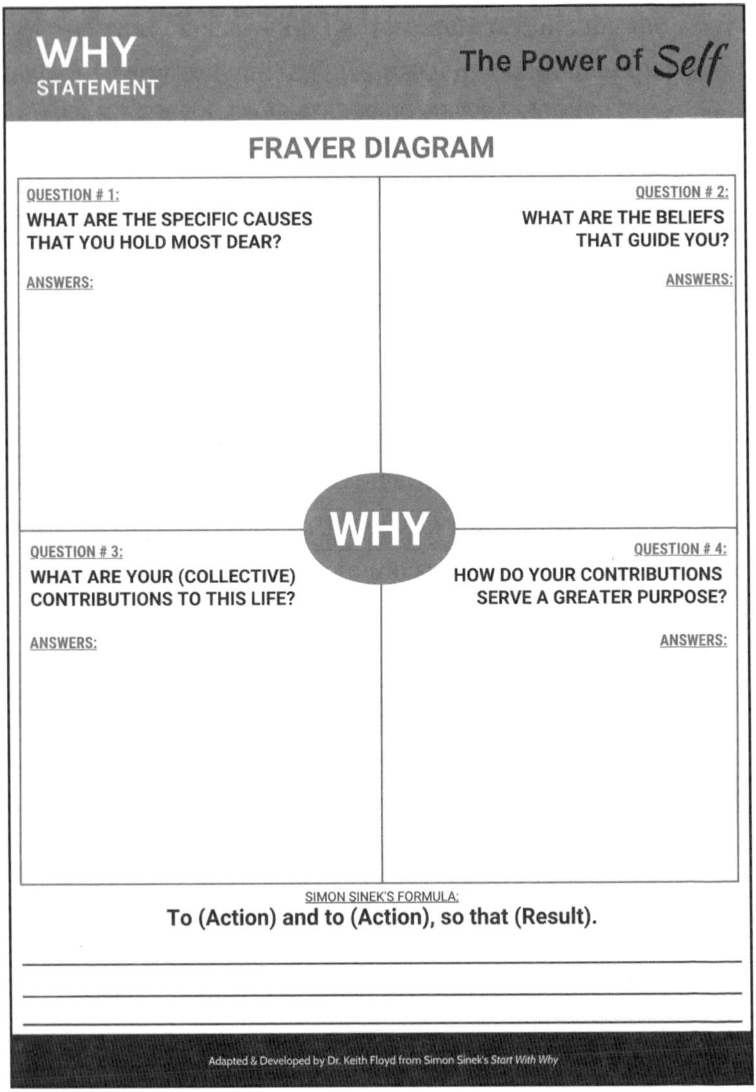

Figure 3.1

You have now collected all the insights and needed information to craft your why statement. The statement should be singular in nature. Despite gathering insights regarding your personal and professional contributions, these reflections and exercises were done to gain greater enlightenment about yourself. Even so, a true *why statement* transcends your personal life and your professional life and is simply a statement for *your life*. But how? To accomplish this final task, you will utilize a formula developed by Simon Sinek. Sinek's simple formula may be found at the bottom of Figure 3.1 and is as follows: *To (Action) and to (Action), so that (Result)*. For example, my personal *why statement* is: To engage with and to cultivate people, so that they may become the persons that they are meant to be.

Developing a purpose or *why statement* is not always easy to do on the first try. As you learned from Simon Sinek, the portion of your brain you are attempting to tap into has a limited capacity for language. This is why you completed all of the previous reflections and work to assist you in gathering your thoughts and word selections in preparation for this final task. A task that will more than likely take multiple tries and just a few different iterations until you come to your final statement. So, how will you know when you have crafted your "true *why* statement?" Simple...it will just "feel right."

Utilizing your responses to questions 1-4 in Figure 3.1, please reread the questions and your responses in sequence (i.e., Question 1 - Responses, Question 2 - Responses, Question 3 – Responses, and Question 4 – Responses). Follow this exact sequence three times in succession and then complete

Reflection 3.4 or the bottom of Figure 3.1.

 **REFLECTION**

1. Simon Sinek's Formula: To (Action) and to (Action), so that (Result).

(Note: After completing your Why Statement, transfer your statement to the bottom of Figure 3.1 or onto the other document option choices referenced earlier or vice versa)

_____

_____

_____

_____

_____

Reflection 3.4

The development of a personal *why statement* is a major accomplishment and one that should not be undervalued. Creating a *why statement* that guides you in all aspects of your life and can be articulated in just a few words is of priceless value and a tremendous accomplishment. An accomplishment that is important to recognize, but at the same time, also recognizing the importance of remaining committed and diligent to honing and re-honing your statement until the statement "feels just right." Until that "just right" statement arrives, take comfort in the fact that even the early iterations that "aren't quite there" still help you demonstrate your true authentic self. A demonstration that is of profound significance.

Your newly created *why statement* solidly places you on your way to "saying and doing the things that you actually believe," a nearly unmeasurable pathway to authenticity. As Simon Sinek states, "Only when that happens [saying and doing the things that you actually believe] can the things you say and do be viewed as authentic." Without the understanding and articulation of your *why*, you risk making countless missteps that could allow you to be seen as inauthentic—a portrayal that is challenging to overcome once established. But that is no longer the case for you. The heartfelt and honest work you have put into yourself and your journey to this point is again nearly priceless. Your newfound *why* will allow you to avoid the missteps that befall those who are not as fully aware of *who they are* and *their why*.

Your why is a powerful resource for you and your journey of discovery. A journey that is an ongoing process of enlightenment, development, and evolution. A process that really and truly has no end—just the next iteration of yourself, and the one after that, and the one after that, and so on. What better way to take such a journey than by knowing who you truly are, how and why you are this way, and why you are here—your purpose for this life. This knowledge of yourself and your *why* in this life—your life's work—is a tremendously noble endeavor with amazing discoveries and outcomes that can come from it. Outcomes like helping to save a fledgling broadcasting company by being your true authentic self while giving children a safe place to learn and grow, as Mr. Rogers did. Or being able to speak from the heart and inspire millions of people to fight a peaceful fight, to rid the world of social and racial injustices. Speaking from the heart and sharing a dream for a future that can be, in a truly authentic way, just as Dr. Martin Luther King Jr. did.

The authentic demonstrations that each of these men put forth allowed each to accomplish seemingly impossible tasks by just being their true selves. Being their authentic selves. Selves that were known to each, and each was willing to be open and honest, and tremendously vulnerable with those in their presence. They were willing to unashamedly share their *why* with the world while remaining confident in their respective pursuits—pursuits that were steadfast because they knew what they needed to do, they knew how to do it, and most importantly, they knew why they were doing it. Their knowledge was gained by their respective journeys of reflection and discovery—discoveries that provided each of them with tremendous strength and conviction. Their strength came from being their true authentic self, along with the conviction to allow that self to be shared with the world, all of which was made possible through their respective self-understanding.

PART 3: SELF-UNDERSTANDING
IN SUMMARY

"To thine own self be true."

William Shakespeare's charge to each and every one of us is timeless and universal, considering these words were written over 400 years ago. Shakespeare's words remain a powerful reminder to guard against being led astray by others, and instead be committed to the principles that drive you and attuned to the *why* that guides you. A *why* that is created by the understanding of your *causes*, your *beliefs*, and your *contributions* to this world.

Your *why* begins with recognizing and acknowledging your causes, that is, the things you "hold most dear." These "most dear" endeavors are the things that motivate you to act. Your own personal and respective calls to action. Actions that are guided by the core pieces of you—*your principles and ideals*. These principles and ideals drive you forward each and every day.

Your *why* is also rooted in much deeper aspects of yourself. Aspects that constitute *your core beliefs*. The beliefs are the things in life that ground you, comprising several walls of your personal foundation that consists of the things, or areas, within your life that you have firm opinions about, or strong convictions to and for. These aspects are the proverbial building blocks that create the foundational walls that the majority of your life is built upon.

These foundational walls are the supports that allow for your respective contributions to be fashioned and gifted.

Contributions to and for others are paid forward employing the totality of who you are as a person. Contributions that transcend the very acts themselves and allow the collective contribution to serve a greater good.

Your personal *why* is an outward projection of who you are and your mission in life. A declaration of the core desires that you wish to accomplish within this lifetime. Accomplishments that are not for personal gain, but for the betterment of others and the world— a world that is better off because of you, your gifts, and the legacy these gifts provide.

SO NOW WHAT?
(ACTION STEPS)

ACTION STEP 1: **YOUR CAUSES**

Your causes are your calls to action. Use the insights gained about your causes, and the endeavors you hold most dear, to move you to action in support of these causes.

ACTION STEP 2: **YOUR BELIEFS**

Use your principles and ideals as a starting point, and then take these core pieces of yourself to the next level through the power of your convictions, and the demonstration of your core beliefs.

ACTION STEP 3: **YOUR *WHY***

Declare your *why*, embody your *why*, and live your *why* every day.

SELF: THE "THREE YOU(s)"

AUTHENTICITY:
THE OUTCOME OF THE POWER OF SELF

*"Discovering the truth about ourselves is
a lifetime's work, but it's worth the effort."*
- Fred Rogers

With the left side of his forehead supported ever so slightly by the heel of his left hand, his elbow resting on the piano right above the keyboard, the slender young man, with his tie held neatly in place at his collar by his metal tie bar, prepares to share his story. As he begins, his voice is calm and perfectly paired with his thoughtful, yet reflective gaze. He began telling the story of the day he visited the new nursery school nearby. He had never been to the school, nor met with the children of the school before, so the encounter was new and unknown. As he walked into the room, there were long stares from many of the children. Then one young boy, Thatcher, spoke up and said, "my doggie's ear came off in the automatic washer." The entire room of children instantly fell silent at the young boy's announcement.

The slender young man paused, feeling as though the young boy had just presented him with a test of honor to see if the young man was still in tune with his own inner child and understood the gravity of this horrible tragedy. The young man said, "Sometimes that happens to toys, doesn't it? Their ears come off, or their legs come off, but that never happens to us. Our ears don't come off; our noses don't come off; our arms don't come off." All the while Thatcher's eyes grew bigger and bigger, and he pronounced, "Our legs don't come off!" The slender young man smiled and said, "No, they don't." Immediately following this exchange, the other children all began to ask questions, very poignant questions to be precise. It was as if the children had opened a door for the gentle, slender young man and were saying, "You have passed the test, and you may now come in."

This very heartfelt and touching exchange occurred between Fred Rogers and the group of preschoolers and was recounted by Fred Rogers himself in the documentary "Won't You Be My Neighbor?"[35] The documentary features his life and story, as well as highlights his remarkable ability to simply be himself in a truly authentic manner at all times. The manner and ease in which he could engage with and connect with almost every single person he met was absolutely amazing. From powerful and influential senators to a preschooler who was lamenting the loss of an ear from one of his most prized possessions, it was extraordinary. A gift of a connection made possible by his own self-awareness and his ability to access all aspects of himself in a truly authentic way.

Fred Rogers was an extraordinary man. A man who gave of himself and displayed his kindness to everyone and everything. His kindness positively impacted those around him and they in turn impacted those around them as well. Each demonstration was real and unabashed in its authenticity and seemed almost superhero-like in nature and too good to be true. But Fred Rogers was not a superhero. He couldn't "leap tall buildings in a single bound," but he could simply be himself. Despite all that he contributed to this world in his life and now in his death, he was simply a man—a man who knew who he was, knew how and why he thought about life, and knew the importance of being himself. A man who knew to his core what he believed in, what his contributions were to this world, and most importantly, why he was on this planet and what his mission in life was to be. It was a powerful combination that allowed him to be himself, *his true, authentic self*. A self that was reflected upon, discovered, and made known, just like you are doing at this moment and through the journey of discovery through this book, and becoming *you* in real time. These are real moments that are giving rise to a *you* that has always been there, but with whom you are just now becoming acquainted. This *you* is the foundation upon which the "newest version" of you is now being built, as well as all of the other versions that are to come in your near and distant future.

But how did you become yourself in the first place? Beyond the obvious act of conception, what was the process that allowed you to be you at this point in your life—reading this book, exploring the various facets of yourself and the world around you, and contemplating what it all means? To understand and answer these deeply profound questions, you must first understand how you became "you" in the first place. What was the process by which you, and nearly every single person on this planet, have traveled and traversed, developmentally speaking, to become who you are today? The *you* that you are is due, in large part, to your respective biology. Biology allows for a series of developmental stages to occur with the outcome being the base upon which you, I, and the vast majority of humanity were and are built.

YOU

Jean Piaget, famed Swiss psychologist, formulated many ground-breaking discoveries during his lifetime of work. Piaget's greatest works and contributions came with children and their respective stages of cognitive development. His contributions helped to explain how people grow and develop from the earliest days of their lives through adulthood. Piaget distinguished and categorized four main stages of development that each of us displays and progresses through during our respective development and lives.

The first stage of development is the Sensory-Motor Stage, "sensory" meaning seeing and hearing, and "motor" meaning reaching and touching, also known as the Preverbal Stage. This stage begins at the day of our birth and lasts on average to around one and a half to two years of age. During the earliest portions of this initial stage, we have no "object permanence," meaning once we (infants) see something disappear, we believe it is gone and will not return. This is why when you play peek-a-boo with a baby, they are so excited and amazed that you have returned once you remove your hands from your face and show your face to them once again. During this stage, we also gather and begin to develop our "Representational Knowledge," or our ability to connect names and words to objects. This initial stage leads to stage two in our cognitive development.

In stage two, or the Pre-Operational Representation Stage, we experience the beginnings of language, initially babbling (with no ability for conversation) with symbolic functions, meaning we see things but are still challenged to equate one thing to another until we develop the ability to mentally display objects in our mind that are not directly visible, and the formation of early thoughts. This second stage progresses with ongoing development in all three of these areas, growing exponentially until around age 7.

The third stage, which occurs between 7 and 11 years of age, is categorized as the Concrete Operational Stage. In this stage, we begin to demonstrate ordering (logic) and spatial recognition (assigning a location and a context of an object).

During this stage, we are able to demonstrate elementary understanding and thinking as they relate to mathematics, geometry, and even physics. This third stage allows us to then move into the fourth and final stage, or the Formal Operational Stage. This final stage begins around the age of 12 and continues to develop as it carries us through the remainder of our adult lives. This fourth and final stage is where reasoning and theoretical/hypothetical thinking develop, that is, the ability to utilize abstract logic and reasoning, and at this stage, strategy and planning become possible, and we are able to transfer context from one situation to another—an application and process that makes much of everyday adult life possible.[36, 37]

These four stages and this process of cognitive development are how you and I each came to be. We are built upon a series of stacked foundational stages of learned behaviors and skills that allow for our respective abilities to develop and then be utilized. The process, specifically in the fourth and final stage, provides us with the opportunity to build and rebuild who we are based upon what we have discovered and learned about ourselves, again just like you are doing at this present moment through your various explorations and purposeful work within this book.

Using Piaget's fourth stage, the Formal Operational Stage, as a framework from the preceding paragraph, let's look at your recent journey and work through the various aspects of this stage. Piaget stated that as we grow and mature in our cognitive development (and abilities) we are better able to reason, employ theoretical/hypothetical thinking, apply abstract logic and reasoning, incorporate strategy and planning into our lives, and demonstrate transference of context from one event to another. To this end, pause, reflect, and complete Reflection 4.1.

 **REFLECTION**

1. **REASON:** What was the reason for your purchase of *The Power of Self* book and embarking on this journey of self-discovery?

_____

_____

_____

_____

_____

2. **EMPLOY THEORETICAL/HYPOTHETICAL THINKING:** If you could have a conversation with yourself 10 years in the future, your "future self," what do you think that version of you would tell you about yourself and what you will discover, realize, learn, and even accomplish during the course of your upcoming 10 years?

_____

_____

_____

_____

_____

3. **APPLY ABSTRACT LOGIC & REASONING:** How will the knowledge gained from 10 years in the future be used by your "future you" between now and then? And what is the reasoning behind the use of each of the insights and learnings?

_____

_____

_____

_____

_____

4. **INCORPORATE STRATEGY & PLANNING:** What will be your specific (detailed) strategy and plan to ensure that your "present you" is able to meet "future you" 10 years from now?

_____

_____

_____

_____

_____

5. **TRANSFERENCE OF CONTEXT FROM ONE EVENT TO ANOTHER:** How will you transfer (execute) your new strategy and plan into action moving forward, basing it upon what you've recently learned about yourself and what is to come in your near and distant future?

_____

_____

_____

_____

_____

Reflection 4.1

This explanation of how you, became you is just a beginning, _not an end._ The _you_ that has developed as Piaget suggests is like a brand-new computer right out of the box. You came equipped with some base circuitry and hardware, as well as some initial base programming and software installed onto it, but without use, experiences, and development, the system will remain a shell of its full potential. A potential that may only be realized with engagement, use, and demonstration, much like you at the present moment. A *you* that grows and evolves into the next stage, the next iteration, of who you truly are and who you are becoming. Becoming a *you* that is being made by means of utilizing exploration, learning, and growth. And a *you* that is constructed and gained from and through knowledge, concept, and understanding. A *you* that is in a constant state of discovery and becoming the next best version of yourself. A *you* that has been discovered through the journey and course of this book. A *discovered you* that will allow you to reach closer to your full potential. A potential that is housed within the confines of *you*. A *you* that is gaining ground each and every day on the "true you." The true *authentic you*. A *you* that sees and processes the world with new eyes and new understanding of yourself and others. An *authentic you* that is being discovered and rediscovered every single day by the work that you have done and the work that you will continue to do. A *you* that is on a course to meet your "future you" 10 years in the future, and then the 10 years in the future beyond that, and so on.

DISCOVERED YOU

In the November 2013 issue of *The Atlantic*, author James

Fallows penned an article entitled "The 50 Greatest Break-throughs Since the Wheel." The article, which was featured in the technology section of the magazine, began with two questions and a statement as an extension of the article's title. Those questions being: "Why did it take so long to invent the wheelbarrow? Have we hit peak innovation? What our list reveals about imagination, optimism, and the nature of progress." Before jumping into the highlights of the list, it is important to have a little more context regarding the construct of the article.

The final list of the 50 greatest breakthroughs was created by a panel of 12 scientists, entrepreneurs, engineers, historians of technology, and others to "assess the innovations that have done the most to shape the nature of modern life." The panel was given the following guidelines:

1. The discoveries, inventions, or innovations should have followed the "widespread use of the wheel" or within the last 6,000 years of human existence, and;

2. Their curated list should include their top 25 choices in rank order of importance.

With these two guidelines in place, the panelists were set to their task.

In the end, despite several of the panelists taking some "liberties" with how they went about categorizing and listing their choices, Fallows sat down with each of the panelists to further discuss the topic of innovation as a whole, while also accomplishing what he set out to do at the onset, that is to compile a collective ranked list (based upon the frequency of the discovery being named and the relative ranking of the collective panelists' responses) of the 50 greatest breakthroughs or discoveries of modern times. Here are a few notable highlights with the ranking, breakthrough, and some insight (according to Fallows or the specified panelist) into the reasoning behind the particular discovery.

RANK: DISCOVERY/BREAKTHROUGH:

#1   The Printing Press (circa 1430) – Panelist George Dyson (technology historian) stated that the printing press was a turning point for humanity because "knowledge began freely replicating and quickly assumed a life of its own."

#9   The Internet (circa 1960) – The Internet is the "infrastructure of the digital age."

#12   Sanitation Systems (circa mid-19th century) – "A major reason we live 40 years longer than we did in 1880."

#16   The Personal Computer (circa 1970) – "It augmented human capabilities."

#27   The Mechanized Clock (circa 15th century) – "It quantified time."

#37   Cement (circa 1st century BCE) – The literal "foundation of civilization."

#40   The Sailboat (circa 4th millennium BCE) – It "transformed travel, warfare, and our view of the world."

#43   The Abacus (circa 3rd century BCE) – "One of the first devices to augment human intelligence."

#50   The Combine Harvester (circa 1930) –
        It "mechanized the farm, freeing people to do new
        types of work."

These are just a sampling of the full list put forth by Fallows through the knowledge, assistance, and expertise of the gathered and esteemed panelists.[38] The full list is intriguing and immensely thought-provoking, and well worth the time for review and reflection. A process of review and reflection similar to another great discovery, the newly *discovered you*. A *you* that is the embodiment of your hard work and personal innovation. A *you* whose breakthrough is allowing for a new *more authentic you*. A *you* that is knowledge-filled, concept-centered, more fully understood, and purpose-driven. A *discovered you* that previously may never have been imagined. A *you* that is now ready to look to the future through new lenses and with newly gained insights and knowledge.

Using the theme and context of Fallows' article title as your guide, specifically: *Imagination, Optimism, and The Nature of Progress*, pause, reflect, and complete Reflection 4.2.

 **REFLECTION**

1. **IMAGINATION:** What do you imagine for yourself moving
   forward due to your work on this journey (and as an extension
   of your conversation with yourself from 10 years in the future)
   and how will this all potentially come to be, due to your now
   newly discovered authentic self?

   _____

   _____

   _____

   _____

   _____

2. **OPTIMISM:** What are you most optimistic about as you look to
   the future? Why are you so optimistic?

   _____

   _____

   _____

   _____

   _____

3. **THE NATURE OF PROGRESS:** What will be the next "natural pro-
   gression" for your newly discovered authentic self? How will it
   align with what you imagined in question # 1 of this Reflection?

   _____

   _____

   _____

   _____

   _____

Reflection 4.2

The answers to the questions posed in Reflections 4.1 and 4.2 are meant to be a stepping-off point for you and the "future you(s)" to come and will initiate an ongoing journey of learning and discovery guided and fueled by what you have learned and continue to learn about yourself. It is a future yet to be written, but at least you now have some insights into what that path may look like: a forward-looking vision that allows you to put into motion purposeful actions and, when coupled with understanding and intent, allows for your future projected realities to become "actual realities."

These realities will be formulated by your discoveries and through the understanding of yourself, and result from the purpose that drives you, and now exist simply because you are "you" in a *truly authentic manner*. This authentic you will be constantly evolving and becoming the next great innovation of the present *you*. To enable this all to occur, you must become and remain driven and diligent in your work and pursuits, and you must be able to gauge your successes and your failures along this journey, all-the-while being able to navigate safely within and around your blind spots as well. You will be navigating into a future that you are crafting and living each and every day. It will be an *authentic you* that will be proud of the work that you've accomplished and the growth that you have made in the months and years ahead. An *authentic you* that will be proud to make the acquaintance of 10 years in the future you, and at which time the "future you" will express their gratitude to you for allowing them to come into being. That meeting will then become the springboard to an even more exciting discussion as to what the 10 years beyond that will hold in store for you, and so on.

AUTHENTIC YOU

In 1995, University of Akron professor Dr. Rebecca Erickson published a research article in *Symbolic Interaction* entitled "The Importance of Authenticity for Self and Society." In the article, Dr. Erickson explored how "the issues of authenticity have become a pervasive part of our culture, our institutions, and our individual selves" in our modern culture and society. Additionally, and building upon the work of the late Dr. Morris Rosenberg and the late Dr. Ralph Turner, Erickson formulated a concept of "authenticity in terms of a commitment to self-values." Dr. Erickson's research and work, even though nearly 30 years in the past, is still quite relevant and moving as it pertains to authenticity and your present journey toward a more authentic you. But first, it is important to gain a little more insight and context from Dr. Erickson's research before going further.

Erickson began her article by citing several other authors and researchers for some context before concluding with her findings. One such context is the difference between "sincerity" and "authenticity." Many times, people will use each of these terms interchangeably, but they are not the same; they are indeed very different. Paraphrasing the late Lionel Trilling, "sincerity" has more to do with how we present ourselves fully and honestly to others, whereas "authenticity" is more about knowing and understanding who we truly are. To accomplish this knowledge and understanding of ourselves, according to Dr. Rosenberg, we must be willing to self-evaluate all aspects of ourselves and our commitments to ourselves by way of our respective values or, as Erickson states, "self-values." And going one step further, quoting Erickson once again, people who "are not fulfilling the commitments they have to self…come to experience feelings of relative inauthenticity." This potential "inauthentic" state is a warning to us all.[39] But how could this occur without our knowing it? Quite easily in fact.

In Part 2 of this book, during your work on self-concept, Dr. Russell Fazio and his colleagues enlightened us to the ease by which each of us can be manipulated into being someone other than our true self—especially in our present-day, social media-saturated, digital culture that is continuously showing and telling us who we ought to be, instead of allowing us to self-discover, and to be who we truly are. All this is to say that your present journey of self-discovery, and in the process the formulation of a more *authentic you*, are a means to an end in unearthing the pieces, aspects, and values that make you—*you* and, in turn, allow you to live a more authentic and, hopefully, more fulfilled life.

In Part 3 of this book, I shared my personal *why* statement with you. The statement is the outward expression of my purpose (my *why*) in life. One of the key expressions or tenets of that statement revolves around the context of the "various persons" model. The idea and model is that we grow into and grow out of various versions of ourselves through our ongoing learning and evolution throughout the course of our life. It is a series of different iterations that are built off the original base model created at the moment of our birth and continue on, moving from one stage to the next, from one version to the next. This compilation of versions then, when sequenced together, provides us with a lifetime of work and experience. It is as Fred Rogers' statement at the onset of this chapter declares, "a lifetime's work" that is well worth doing and "worth the effort." A life that we hope to be fulfilled in living, due to our knowledge, concept, and understanding that then gives way to an even deeper, more authentic self that has arisen from your current exploration and deep work, and, in the process, has left the previous, less knowledgeable version of you and the accompanying remnants in the past.

This past self is very different from the person you are now due to your investment of time, self-reflection, and intense thought. It is a *present you* that knows much more about yourself than the *former you* who first opened this book some time ago and was presented with a simple three-word question at the onset of the book, which was a simple question that possibly stopped the former you dead in your tracks because the former you did not have the benefit of the insights, learnings, and growth that the *current you* now possesses. This newest version of you is now much better prepared to tackle that simple three-word question with greater ease and confidence than your predecessor, and tackling that will be the final reflection within the confines of this book, and your current journey.

Take a moment to pause, reflect, and complete Reflection 4.3. Answer the simple three-word question, but this time with the self-knowledge, self-concept, and self-understanding you now possess.

 REFLECTION

1. SIMPLE THREE-WORD QUESTION: Who are you?

I am: _____

_____

_____

_____

_____

_____

_____

_____

_____

_____

_____

_____

_____

_____

_____

_____

_____

_____

_____

_____

_____

_____

_____

_____

Reflection 4.3

In answering this now familiar three-word question, you are more than likely beginning to fully appreciate the journey you have recently been on, while also realizing that a journey of this type, a journey of personal self-discovery, truly has no end. For the end of whatever stage of the journey you are currently on is simply the stepping stone to the next stage or leg of the journey. This realization unto itself is truly what *The Power of Self* is all about. It is about awareness. It is about discovery. It is about change. A change that is ongoing. Ongoing in that you should be continuously learning about yourself and striving to become that next best version of yourself. A version that will eventually be trumped by the version after that and the one after that. With each version eclipsing the one prior.

The eclipsing version will have even more self-knowledge, a stronger self-concept, and even greater self-understanding than the version of you that preceded it. And when the time comes, a time that eventually comes for all of us, when your life's journey is destined to be in its final and last leg, the conclusion of a life's odyssey, at that moment, at least you will know that you have worked hard to be the best you, your *authentic you*, all along the way. In doing so, you will have presented the world with a tremendous gift. The gift of *your true authentic self*. A gift that others will be honored and feel privileged to have received. These recipients are the literal and proverbial neighbors in your respective neighborhood that is filled with caring, understanding, and authentic individuals— much like the neighborhood crafted and created by Mr. Rogers.

Fred Rogers worked tirelessly throughout the entirety of

his career and life to be authentic and to express himself in an authentic manner, day in and day out. Fred Rogers' ability to be his *authentic self* was truly a testament to his self-knowledge. He put forth the best of himself in a straightforward and unapologetic manner. A demonstration of caring and self that was absolutely from the heart and was genuine and authentic at all times, and a constant display of who he truly was that left him (at times) open to being the recipient of various jokes and parodies. Even so, Fred Rogers never wavered. He knew what he stood for. He knew what he believed in and that being who he was, was the only way he could be. This unwavering commitment to himself, his beliefs, and his "self-values" is the cornerstone of authenticity.

The ability to be who you are because it is the only way that you know how to be. With this description, Fred Rogers, by all accounts, was a truly authentic human being in every moment, and in every setting, no matter if he was talking to a room full of preschoolers, standing before a sea of college students on their graduation day delivering their commencement address, or centerstage before a committee of prominent and influential politicians. It made no difference. He was the man he was, and he was authentic in every way.

PART 4: THE POWER OF SELF
IN SUMMARY

The *"who"* you are today started at the moment of your birth. All of the nuances and traits that make you who *you* are have been a life's journey to this point. But as you have just found out through this book, it does not have to be the destination, but simply the next stage or leg to becoming the next iteration of your true authentic self.

The ability to know what you believe in, what your contributions are to this world, and most importantly, why you are on this planet, and what your mission in life is to be, is a powerful combination that allows for your authentic self to come into being. But all of this does not occur by happenstance. We all travel and traverse our respective journeys, developmentally speaking, nearly the same way.

It all begins with our birth, and we all (mostly) move through the same stages, of which there are four, to becoming who we are, biologically and developmentally speaking. In each of these stages we develop, learn, and grow as people. Within the fourth and final stage, The Formal Operational Stage, is when you are able to begin to think more fully: reason, employ theoretical/hypothetical thinking, apply abstract logic and reasoning, incorporate strategy and planning into your life, and demonstrate transference of context from one event to another. These are just a few of the aspects that allow you to begin discovering your true, authentic self.

The discovery of your new authentic self is largely due to your journey thus far and has been accomplished through your hard work and deep reflection. The newly discovered you is, to a greater extent, more knowledge-filled, concept-centered, and more fully understood and purpose-driven than the previous versions of yourself. A discovered *you* who is now ready to look to the future through new lenses and with newfound insights and knowledge. A discovered *you* upon whom all future "authentic you(s)" will be built and developed.

The journey toward, and the discovery of, your true authentic self is a lifelong endeavor. It is an endeavor that will allow you to continuously become the "persons" that you are meant to be while also helping to make the world an even better place due to your authentic self being out in front and leading the way.

SO NOW WHAT?
(ACTION STEPS)

ACTION STEP 1: **YOU**

Use your abilities for theoretical/hypothetical thinking, abstract logic and reasoning, and strategy and planning to continually be looking toward the future—say 10 years—so that your current and future authentic selves are able to meet when the time comes.

ACTION STEP 2: **DISCOVERED YOU**

Building off of your forward-thinking skills and abilities, challenge yourself to constantly search for and discover the next best version of your authentic self in the here and now.

ACTION STEP 3: **AUTHENTIC YOU**

Now that you are able to fully and completely answer the question "Who are you?" live each and every day as your true authentic self.

CLOSING

BEING YOUR AUTHENTIC SELF

This book, as you may have guessed by now, is a collection of lessons that I have learned while traveling throughout this wonderful, sometimes challenging, amazing life. It is my sincere hope that you, as well as anyone who reads this book, understand that this book is intended to be my gift to you. I hope this gift allows you to gain some of the same self-knowledge, self-concept, and self-understanding that I have gained throughout the course of my life and through my journeys to this point. The knowledge and insights I have gained have taught and assisted me both personally and professionally and have led me to this exact moment in time. It is these gifts that I now pass on to you so that you may now explore the world with a whole new set of understandings, and through a whole new set of lenses, which will in turn (at least I hope that they will) inspire you to continue to challenge yourself to learn as much as you possibly can about who you truly are and what wonderous things you have to offer this world, and this life.

As I have shared many times throughout the course of this book, and I feel compelled to state it yet once again—this book (especially now at the conclusion) should not be seen as an end to your present journey, not even in the slightest. On the contrary, it should be an exhilarating stepping off point where this new version of yourself is ready to be shared with the world by way of your newfound authentic self. A new self that may, and will, become a role model for others as you demonstrate your true self to them day after day, and time after time. And through this demonstration, hopefully, they too will become inspired to learn who they truly are so that they too may strive to become the next best versions of themselves. In this demonstration, you will have "paid it forward" by gifting your authentic self to them, as well as the world around them, by simply being *you*. A *you* that is now in the early days of your newest explorations to becoming the even newer, even better, next best version of yourself.

So, as you prepare to step out and step off on your new adventure and begin to show the world who you truly are, I would like to leave you with some insights from one of my favorite pieces of literature. A piece of literature not written by Plato, Aristotle, or Shakespeare, but instead put forth by one of the greatest children's authors of all time. An individual who, just like Mr. Rogers, also had a love for children and wished to prepare them for life through the lessons contained in his writings, just as Fred Rogers did through his television programs. This author was a man who gave us similar lessons for life, but instead of puppets or songs, he used verse and rhyme. A giant of literature and very much a kindred spirit to Mr. Rogers. So, who is this giant of literature? None other than Theodor Seuss Geisel or Dr. Seuss.

Theodor Seuss Geisel (Dr. Seuss), was a writer and illustrator who created more than 60 entertaining and enlightening works of art. His books are filled with valuable lessons that make readers laugh, think, and feel inspired to explore new worlds. In his final work, "Oh, The Places You'll Go," Dr. Seuss encourages us to embrace life and all of its ups and downs. Even when things get tough, we must stay motivated and never give up on our hopes and dreams.[40] These powerful sentiments are meant to inspire and guide us forward. Inspirations and pathways much like your own explorations and discoveries as you continue to unearth and meet the future versions of yourself, while living out *The Power of Self.*

For downloadable PDF versions of all activities and exercises within this book, visit:

www.ThePowerofSelfbook.com

ENDNOTES

OPENING:

1. Rogers, F. (May 1969). May 1, 1969: *Fred Rogers Testifies Before The Senate Subcommittee on Communications*. [Video]. YouTube. https://www.youtube.com/watch?v=fKy7ljRr0AA.

2. John Pastore. (2021. March 6). In *Wikipedia*. https://en.wikipedia.org/wiki/John_Pastore.

3. Patinkin, M. (2017, May 31). Mark Patinkin: "Recalling when Mister Rogers softened a tough Rhode Island senator." *Providence Journal*. https://www.providencejournal.com/news/20170531/mark-patinkin-recalling-when-mister-rogers-softened-tough-rhode-island-senator.

4. Strachan, M. (2017, March 16). "The Best Argument for Saving Public Media was Made By Mr. Rogers in 1969." *Huffington Post*. https://www.huffpost.com/entry/mr-rogers-pbs-budget-cuts_n_58ca8d6fe4b0be71dcf1d440.

SELF – PART 1:

5. Bollich, K., Johannet, P., Vazire, S.. (2011). "In search of our true selves: feedback as a path to self-knowledge," *Frontiers in Psychology*, Vol. 2. Article 312. (November 2011).

6. Best, K. (2018, August 7). "Know Thyself: The Philosophy of Self-Knowledge." *UConn Today* (University of Connecticut). https://today.uconn.edu/2018/08/know-thyself-philosophy-self-knowledge.

7. Perdue, S. M. (2014, September 19). "The Big 3 of Greek Philosophy: Socrates, Plato, and Aristotle." *English Blog* (Penn State University). https://sites.psu.edu/rclperdue/2014/09/19/the-big-three-of-greek-philosophy-socrates-plato-and-aristotle.

8. Bollich, K., Johannet, P., Vazire, S.. (2011). "In search of our true selves: feedback as a path to self-knowledge," *Frontiers in Psychology*, Vol. 2. Article 312. (November 2011).

9. Gallup and Rath (2007). *StrengthsFinder 2.0*. Gallup Press.

10. Gallup, Inc. (2000). *Strengths: Brief Theme Descriptions*. PDF File.

11. Isaacson, W. (2011). *Steve Jobs: The Exclusive Biography*. Simon & Schuster.

12. "Volvo Car Corporation Presents World-First Systems for Improved Safety." Press Release [January 5, 2004], from https://www.media.volvocars.com/global/en-gb/media/pressreleases/4923.

13. "Blind-Spot Information System." Retrieved [April 24, 2021], from https://www.loveringconcord.com/blind-spot-information-system.htm.

14. M. A. Sotelo, J. Barriga, D. Fernández, I. Parra, J. E. Naranjo, M. Marrón et al. (2007). "Vision-Based Blind Spot Detection Using Optical Flow. Computer Aided Systems Theory – Eurocast 2007." (p. 1113-1118).

15. Bollich, K., Johannet, P., Vazire, S.. (2011). "In search of our true selves: feedback as a path to self-knowledge," *Frontiers in Psychology*, Vol. 2. Article 312. (November 2011).

16. Hamachek, D. (2000). "Dynamics of Self-Understanding and Self-Knowledge: Acquisition, Advantages, and Relation to Emotional Intelligence," *The Journal of Humanistic Counseling, Education and Development*, Vol. 38. Issue 4. (p. 230–242).

17. Schlesinger, A.M. (1959). "Our Ten Contributions to Civilization," *The Atlantic*, Vol. 203. No. 3.

18. Vazire, S., & Carlson, E. N. (2011). "Others sometimes know us better than we know ourselves." *Current Directions in Psychological Science*, 20(2), 104-108.

19. "Who is Nelson Mandela?" *A Reader's Digest* exclusive interview. Retrieved [January 13, 2022], from https://www.rd.com/list/who-is-nelson-mandela-a-readers-digest-exclusive-interview/.

20. Gladwell, M. (2006). *The tipping point: How little things can make a big difference*. Little, Brown.

SELF – PART 2:

21. Fazio, R. H., Effrein, E. A., & Falender, V. J. (1981). "Self-perceptions following social interaction." *Journal of Personality and Social Psychology*, 41(2), 232.

22. Snyder, M., & Swann, W. B. (1978). "Hypothesis-testing processes in social interaction." *Journal of personality and social psychology*, 36(11), 1202.

23. "Self-Perception Theory in Social Psychology." Retrieved [January 29, 2022], from http://psychology.iresearchnet.com/social-psychology/social-psychology-theories/self-perception-theory/.

24. "An Overview of Self-Concept Theory." Retrieved [January 29, 2022], from https://cyc-net.org/cyc-online/cyconline-nov2008-eric.html.

25. "Mind Styles-Anthony Gregorc." Retrieved [January 29, 2022], from https://web.cortland.edu/andersmd/learning/gregorc.htm.

26. "Nails on a Chalkboard." Retrieved [February 9, 2022], from https://www.definition-of.com/nails+on+a+chalkboard.

27. "Rorschach Inkblot Test: Definition, History & Interpretation." Retrieved [February 26, 2022], from https://www.simplypsychology.org/what-is-the-rorschach-inkblot-test.html.

28. Peshkin, A. (2001). "Angles of vision: Enhancing perception in qualitative research." *Qualitative Inquiry*, 7(2), 238-253.

29. Rogers, C. R. (1975). "Empathic: An unappreciated way of being." *The Counseling Psychologist*, 5(2), 2-10.

SELF – PART 3:

30. "What are Shakespeare's Most Famous Quotes?" Retrieved [March 8, 2022], from https://www.biography.com/news/shakespeares-most-famous-quotes.

31. Bloom, H. (1998). *Shakespeare: The Invention of the Human*. Riverdale Books.

32. Sinek, S. (2009). *Start With Why: How great leaders inspire everyone to take action*. Penguin.

33. Simon Sinek – "How Great Leaders Inspire Action." TEDxPuget Sound. September 2009. https://www.ted.com/talks/simon_sinek_how_great_leaders_inspire_action?language=en.

34. 1964 Nobel Peace Prize. Retrieved [March 10, 2022], from https://www.nps.gov/malu/planyourvisit/1964-nobel-peace-prize.htm.

152

SELF – PART 4:

35. Capotosto, C., Ma, N., Neville, M., Rogers, J., Cephas, M., Jr., Clemmons, F., & Rogers, F. (2018). *Won't you be my neighbor?* Universal City, CA: Focus Features.

36. So, I. (1964). "Cognitive development in children: Piaget development and learning." *Journal of Research in Science Teaching*, 2, 176-186.

37. "Piaget's 4 Stages of Cognitive Development Explained." Retrieved [July 17, 2022], from https://www.verywellmind.com/piagets-stages-of-cognitive-development-2795457.

38. Fallows, J. (2013). "The Greatest Breakthroughs Since the Wheel."

39. Erickson, R. J. (1995). "The importance of authenticity for self and society." *Symbolic Interaction*, 18(2), 121-144.

CLOSING:

40. Seuss, Dr. (1990). *Oh, the places you'll go!* New York: Random House.

Still Looking For More?

Learn more about the author and contact him by visiting www.DrKeithFloyd.com.